W9-AGT-900

In the Early Times

IN THE
EARLY TIMES

A LIFE REFRAMED

TAD FRIEND

CROWN
NEW YORK

Portions of this book appeared, in different form, in *The New Yorker.*

Grateful acknowledgment is made to Grove/Atlantic, Inc. and The
Wylie Agency LLC for permission to reprint "Late Fragment" from *A
New Path to the Waterfall* by Raymond Carver. Copyright © 1989 by the
Estate of Raymond Carver. Copyright © 1989, 2000 by Tess Gallagher.
Reprinted by permission of Grove/Atlantic and The Wylie Agency LLC.

Excerpt of "The Hurley Player" from *More Songs from Leinster* by
Winifred M. Letts, originally published in Great Britain by
John Murray, a division of Hachette UK, London, in 1926.

Library of Congress Cataloging-in-Publication Data
Names: Friend, Tad, author.
Title: In the early times / by Tad Friend.
Description: First edition. | New York : Crown, [2022]
Identifiers: LCCN 2021053378 (print) | LCCN 2021053379 (ebook) |
ISBN 9780593137352 (hardcover) | ISBN 9780593137369 (ebook)
Subjects: LCSH: Friend, Tad. | Friend, Tad—Family. | Friend,
Theodore—Last years. | Father and son. | Friend family. |
WASPs (Persons)—Biography.
Classification: LCC CT275.F715 A3 2022 (print) |
LCC CT275.F715 (ebook) | DDC 929.20973—dc23/eng/20211202
LC record available at https://lccn.loc.gov/2021053378
LC ebook record available at https://lccn.loc.gov/2021053379

Printed in the United States of America on acid-free paper

crownpublishing.com

2 4 6 8 9 7 5 3 1

First Edition

Most photos in the book courtesy of Amanda Hesser and Tad Friend.
Additional photos by Margaret "Baba" Dunn (pp. 33, 181, and 240),
Anneliese Garver (p. 54), Karen Z. Pierson (pp. 109, 177, and 210),
and Sara Press (p. 38).

For Amanda

Contents

Author's Note

I have changed the names of Melanie, Phyllis, Martha, and those in the Group, including Paul Klein.

In the Early Times

Hunger

STRANGERS OFTEN told me how wonderful my father was. *Wait, my father?* I'd think. They met a different man, the handsome polymath with the much-stamped passport. The earnest charmer. At conference dinners, he'd linger over the Sauternes to draw out his seatmate's knowledge of Persian poetry; once, with a Korean who spoke almost no English, he was able to convey baseball's arcane balk rule using only pantomime. His pockets were always full of business cards inscribed with pleas to keep in touch, as if he were a human Wailing Wall.

Theodore Wood Friend III was "Dorie" to his contemporaries and "Day" to his children, from my first tries at "Daddy." (We're one of those Wasp families where baby names stick for life.) A believer in letters to the editor and global rapport, he drove four hundred miles to witness Martin Luther King's "I Have a Dream" speech, won the Bancroft Prize for his history of the Philippines three years later, and became president of Swarthmore College,

in 1973, at forty-two. By then, he'd taught the histories of
India, Pakistan, Bangladesh, China, Japan, Korea, and all of
Southeast Asia, as well as of American foreign relations. He
possessed a resonant baritone and a self-deprecating manner, and hopes were high.

The middle years . . . middling. Nudged out at Swarthmore, he sought a spot on Reagan's National Security Council, hoping for a rise to the cabinet from there. After being
passed over, he ran the Eisenhower Exchange Fellowship.
EEF brought foreign go-getters to the United States to
exchange ideas—and, under Day's leadership, began sending Americans overseas for the same purpose. Like America,
he had a missionary temperament, and his sweeping doc-
trines applied even to the three of us children, the smallest
of tribes.

After twelve years at EEF he stepped down, at sixty-five,
to take care of our mother, Elizabeth. If Day was a gravel
truck juddering off to mend the broken world, Mom was a
coupe cornering at speed. At his retirement dinner, where
she wore an auburn wig after her chemo, we all had our
photo taken with two of the foundation's chairmen: Ger-
ald Ford and George H. W. Bush. When the photographer
pointed out that Mom's hand was obscuring Bush's thigh,
Bush remarked, roguishly, "Leave it, Elizabeth, it feels good
where it is."

"That kind of photo costs more, George," she shot back.
Day's guffaw made everyone except Jerry Ford crack up,
and that photo was the keeper.

One August afternoon in 2018, after lunch and before Day's
nap, my younger sister, Timmie, and I sat down with him

in his living room to ask about his life. It felt like our last chance to understand him; he was nearly eighty-six and his once-lush conversation was as clenched as winter wheat. He clearly mistrusted our agenda. The way he sat in his blue armchair—chin low, lips tight, gray hair batwinging from his enormous head—called to mind a nineteenth-century caricature: Boss Tweed astride his empire; the cantankerous Tories.

We began gently, at the beginning, which was probably a mistake, as he hated his Pittsburgh boyhood. Being raised by old-school Wasps was like being raised by a minibar. Timmie asked, "How would your parents have described you?"

"They would have described me as a baby. And then they would have described me as a boy." Timmie glanced over: *Uh-oh.* He was just checking the box: *I owe my children this courtesy*. I was of like mind, a paramedic filling out the forms: *Did you take every possible measure?* I'd suppressed my expectations for so long it felt like a form of filial piety. But Timmie still hoped he might finally confess that he loved us more deeply than, for secret reasons, he could ever reveal.

He closed his eyes and said, "I'm sort of hungry for ice cream."

"You had some a short while ago," she said.

"I did?"

"Right after lunch."

He frowned. Day loved sweets. In college, he got fired from a summer job for filling doughnuts with too much jelly. When we lived in Manila, in 1967, he spent two days in a hospital, as Mom noted in a doleful letter home, "under observation for—you won't believe it—chewing up and swallowing a *Christmas tree ball*! We had a rather elaborate cake in the shape of a dragon and the eyes were glass balls. Dorie thought they were candy and ate one." Two years later, Day wrote Mom from Amsterdam to say, "Drinking 'young gin' (tough) rather than lemon gin (a little sweet) because I want the waiter to realize I am TOUGH. Of course, *you* realize, my lovely, that I am at least a little sweet. I like a lot of brown sugar on my cereal and a lot of white sugar in my tea and a lot of sympathy in my boyish disconsolations."

He was prey to darker desires, too, but he hid those better. Timmie tried again: "If somebody wrote your parents and said, 'Tell us about your son, what's he like?' what would they have said?"

"Nobody did that." His laugh was a rueful bark. "Nobody cared."

"So no one cared about you when you were young?"

"Well, I cared about myself." He laughed again, more softly. "But, no." He turned his reading lamp to glare the bulb at us. You go to the station to file a missing person report, and suddenly you're the suspect.

Whenever I see a father hug his son on-screen I begin to cry. I know. I'm not crazy about it, either; a hug is cinematic mush on the level of a lost dog bounding home. And I cry at that, too! The father doesn't even have to be the son's actual dad; a prisoner on the lam with a kidnapped boy, like Kevin Costner in *A Perfect World*, works just fine—a father *figure*.

My father hugged me until I was about seven. Then he stopped; I don't know why. We started up again when I was in my mid-twenties, because I hugged my friends and I hugged my mom and it seemed weird not to hug my dad. But trying to reach him always felt like ice fishing.

In my earliest recurrent dream, I'd find myself in a meadow that sloped uphill to a door set in a knoll. As I struggled through the tall grass, I'd hear banjo music behind the door; after work, my father had gone there to play. When I grasped the doorknob, though, the music would stop. I'd run among the small bare rooms, then return to the doorway, bewildered. Eventually the banjo would resume, far away. But there was always a door between us.

I tried to turn Day, heeling wide: "What do you think you're best at?"

"I think I am best at . . . listening."

Okay. "How do you feel you've contributed to the world?"

"Three children."

I glanced at Timmie, an interior designer who has Mom's darting humor and radiant smile. Born six years after me, she effectively grew up in a separate wing of the house; we got close only later. "Want to elaborate, at all?" I asked.

"Three beautiful, marvelous, exquisite, wonderful, unique children!" he bellowed.

Shooting me a deadpan look—*Yay, us!*—Timmie asked, "Is there anything you wish you'd done?"

"I wish I'd been president," Day said.

"President of the United States?"

"Yes." He enjoyed naming the presidents in order. "And I wish I'd played music, especially the guitar. All I ever did was turn on the phonograph."

"I never knew that," I said. "I wish I'd played the guitar, too." My children took lessons for years, but, nah. We're the anti–Partridge Family.

Day looked at his watch, then added, "I wish I'd written more creatively. I wish I'd written more fiction." In the eighties, he published a well-received novel about his youth, *Family Laundry*. For years he'd been working on a final book, a memoir.

Timmie asked, "Is there anything you wish you'd spent *less* time doing?"

"Answering questionnaires," he said. "I've answered hundreds of them." He backhanded our question away.

Since Mom died, in 2003, Day has lived alone in their house in Villanova, a leafy, DUI-friendly Philadelphia suburb. These days he has a bookkeeper and a care manager and round-the-clock aides to coax him out of bed and make him comfort food. My family—my wife, Amanda, and our twelve-year-old twins, Addison and Walker—and Timmie and her family had come to be with him for a few days. He mostly sat at the dinner table, reading the *Times* and scowling at commotion. Waking from a catnap, he'd grimace to find himself surrounded by walkers and grip bars and stair lifts and toilet commodes, the paraphernalia of decline. When he went to a rehab facility after one of his hospital stays, he'd begin his care conferences by saying, "Please be candid—I am not an expert in me," then glower at the nurses who announced his "inability to transfer" and need for help with "lower-body bathing" and "self-cleaning management." He'd been so careful to greet them brightly: "Good morning, Kaila/Judith/

Shani!" *I am perfectly well and do not belong here.* He'd pictured an old age lolling by the pond at the foot of his backyard, dispensing breadcrumbs to the koi and wisdom to us. He told us so in 2008, as he distributed copies of his do-not-resuscitate form.

He was able to maintain that seigneurial deportment for years, greeting me heartily when we arrived—"Taddio! How's the man?"—and launching into an account of a recent conclave. When he detailed the workings of one of his boards or institutes or interfaith groups, he'd get side-tracked so often that Timmie and I adopted a shorthand for his digressions. "Billy Grassie" marked a byway of cre-dentialism, and "Metanexus" a plunge into the metaphysi-cal weeds. "My friend Billy Grassie," he'd remind us, "is the founding director of the Metanexus Institute, a kind of *agora*, or marketplace, where scientific inquiry and reli-gious belief can wrestle with each other in mutually play-ful and profitable exchange. Well, Billy is a very able fellow with a PhD in religion. . . ." Day classified everyone he knew as "able" or "very able," enumerated their "vectors of inquiry," and situated them as "a very bright economics PhD from Yale" or "a keen thinker on cross-cultural folk-ways and the first Marshall Scholar from Guam." As con-versation it was broccoli, but there was a Meatless Monday comfort to it: nothing had gone badly wrong yet.

Our brother, Pier, the middle child—a six-foot-five dog lover, athletic and equable—doesn't use our shorthand. His solicitude about Day underlines their resemblance: They wear fleeces, love math, and prize order. Pier, an exec at an investment firm, had come down with his family the week-end before, asked Day no bruising questions, and left him in a better mood than when he'd arrived. Pier's steadiness mystifies me, as he, too, was deeply stamped by Mom's outlook; her catchphrases, such as "Smiling the boy fell dead," were rescue signals disguised as proclamations of buoyancy. *Not waving but drowning.* In 2005, Timmie had a liver transplant. When she awoke eleven hours later in the ICU, we told her the doctors said she was doing very well. From under her leaded blanket of anesthesia, she murmured, "I . . . aim . . . to . . . please," an entirely Mom-ish remark.

Day, who loved bathroom humor and had a booming laugh, could be witty on occasion. His index to his Bancroft-winning *Between Two Empires* contains an entry about the emotional reactions of various Filipino politicians that sneaks in a reference to Mom and her behavior as he was writing the book: "Tears: shed by Quezon, 51; shed by Laurel, 212; shed by Osmeña, 236, 237; shed by Elizabeth, passim"—or throughout. But he almost never made fun of himself.

He's not going to start now. When we arrived, the day before, he was in the bathroom swearing at his caregivers— "Fuck! Don't yank at me!"—his voice squawking over the baby monitor on the kitchen counter. When his care manager asked if he was in pain, he cried, "I'm in *emotional* pain!" And when his cane slid off his chair with a bang, he awoke and roared "Goddammit!" at Timmie, because she was nearest. Newly vulnerable, he is more determined than ever not to be.

When Day poisoned his tea with five heaping spoonfuls of sugar, Addison warned him that his teeth would fall out and that he'd get diabetes—one of her periodic public service announcements denouncing meat, cigarettes, and hypocrisy. He just scowled at her. She scoops out half his sugar when he's not looking, but he recoups it later in cookies. He doesn't fret about getting diabetes because he has leukemia, and he doesn't fret about having leukemia because he is determined to be a stoic, and he doesn't fret about failing to be a stoic because he doesn't always remember that that's what he's supposed to be.

Day at his dinner table.

At lunch, I'd tried to start Day reminiscing by recalling how he'd taught me to skip stones across a creek near Buffalo, where we grew up.

Walker said, "I don't get how that works, Grand-Day." He's determined to beat my record of eleven skips.

"You keep your forearm parallel to the water"—he set his wrist and pronated his forearm—"and you flip a flat stone—"

"No," Walker said, "I mean how the stone skips across the water so many times without sinking." He cocked his head. Like his grandfather's, it's larger than you might reasonably expect.

Day reflected. At times, now, he seems to want to lay his great, heavy brain down. "I am conversant with the art, not the science," he said at last. One of his best memories was when he was seven or eight, and his mother showed him how to skim a stone across a pond. "Watch!" she called, and her stone skittered over in four ricochets. "My miraculous mother," he later wrote. "I was filled with happiness. As I grew older, I felt challenged by any flat body of water to find a skippable stone."

When we'd left Brooklyn to drive to Villanova, I'd eyed the twins in the rearview mirror: Walker, as usual, was taking everything in while seeming to stare out the window; Addison was pouched in a blanket, only her eyes and her cat's-ears headband visible. She lowered the blanket to give me a smile.

Amanda plugged her iPhone into the dash to map the fastest way: there are forks to choose—Hamilton Parkway or the BQE? Goethals or Outerbridge?—and I relish saving even five minutes. Sheryl Crow's recording of "The First Cut Is the Deepest" began playing, as by some quirk of Amanda's iTunes it does whenever she launches Google Maps, and Walker and Addison sang along. The treacly tune had become our rental-car soundtrack. Amanda and I took it up in time for the throaty yearning:

> *Baby, I'll try to love again, but I knowww . . .*
> *The first cut is the deepest, baby, I knowwwww . . .*

As we zipped past the office parks of the Jersey exurbs, I saw Walker resting his head on Addison's lap. She was stroking his hair. I touched Amanda's hand and flicked my eyes back, and she glanced around casually. When our children sense parental doting or Instagramming, they behave like an old-time mercantile partnership asked for a donation: the blinds drop and the locks snick shut. Amanda, who's determined to preserve them at each poignant stage, has taken thousands of photos of them alone and together. "You'll thank me later!" she says, when they fuss and groan.

She herself often radiates inwardness, that unselfaware quality photographers hope to catch. My enduring images of Amanda are mental snapshots: the intent way she cups my face with both hands, then eases in with an eye-on-object focus, only at last parting her lips. The precise way she positions a heavy pillow atop her head to spatchcock herself into sleep, then slips one foot outside the bedcovers as a thermoregulator. The ebullient way she measures Walker and Addison against the pantry cupboard, elated by debatable gains since she measured them two days earlier.

The all-in way she plays basketball for her urban-league team, the Foulmouths—boxing out, double-teaming, scrapping for loose balls. The brisk way she chest-passes laundry into the washing machine, then gives it a nod and a smile: *Go get clean and I'll see you soon!*

Our friends view me as even-keeled, calm in a crisis, a counterbalance to Amanda's excitability, a perception Amanda shares, mostly. I often wonder how our children see me. Is the father I wanted the father they want, too? Or is the father I got the father I've inevitably become?

Walker seems unusually self-possessed: he sits at the cool kids' lunch table, a confidant who reserves judgment. Descending from his upper bunk for breakfast, he floats his feet halfway down the ladder and then nods back off. He required his baby teeth to drop on their own—no twisting or wiggling—and never left them for the tooth fairy: "I'm not selling part of myself for a dollar!" Instead, he hid them in the saltcellar, a tiny china chicken on our dinner table. He hates hikes and museums because they encourage dawdling. Obsessed with sports, he loves to discuss Saka's passing skills or the fortunes of Nike, the most glorious empire known to man. His other treasures emerge obliquely. When Amanda and I fight, it is Walker who steps in as a teary referee.

While he keeps being replaced, in rapid match cuts, by new actors playing taller Walkers, Addison has remained a waif. Happiest racing through the Hunger Games books for the fourth time, she often has no idea what month it is, or where that month falls in the year, guessing that February follows October in the same way she hazards that Idaho is a country. When she tries a deadpan look for a selfie she cracks up at the idea that anyone would voluntarily drain her expression of animation. In this she takes after Amanda, who always has a relaxed smile for the camera, while I usually look like mug-shot Gary Busey.

Addison is a brooder. Mildly obsessive-compulsive— cupboards are ritually caressed, furniture reflexively peeked under—she has worn her cat's-ears headband day and night for nearly three years to prevent an IED from blowing up our family. She gets stomachaches, and then she gets stomachaches from worrying that she's going to get stomachaches. Like my mother, whom she takes after to an extraordinary degree, she's a perfectionist prone to depression. Amanda recently found her at the kitchen table at 2:30 A.M., her head buried in her homework.

Amanda, for her part, had awoken tense with worry and gone to the bathroom to find that the toilet wasn't flushing—and the kids' toilet wasn't, either! After coaxing Addison into bed, she emailed everyone in the building and constructed a "Climate change has swamped the water tunnels and shattered our sewage pipes!" scenario that kept her up till dawn. She regularly patrols our apartment, worried that the stove may spontaneously ignite or that a burglar might be hiding in the four-inch cranny under our bed. War-gaming these premonitions, she'll round the corner, see a stranger, and jump in alarm. *It's just me, your husband.*

Three days later, she texted me, "What's the novel about the looming cloud? The wife wears a sweatsuit."

"*White Noise,*" I replied. "Why? Is your mind taking a doomy turn?"

Silence.

Walker, Addison, and Amanda in Indonesia, 2018.

As a writer for *The New Yorker*, I love portraying outliers: a Hollywood agent who doesn't schmooze; a venture capitalist who relishes the limelight; scientists who believe in the possibility of immortality. In order to understand the rules the rebels are breaking as well as those they're trying to establish, I ask about everything.

This approach works best with strangers. In my family, questions are traditionally limited to how you slept and whether you unloaded the dishwasher yet. Still, you'd think that by now, in my mid-fifties, after years of observation, I'd have a fix on my closest relatives. But fitting your family together begins as a jigsaw puzzle and becomes an anxiety dream. You assemble the exterior first, the frame—your

parents and your own childhood—and your pattern matching improves as you work the pieces, amassing colors and
motifs. Yet the central portrait, of your own marriage and
children, keeps shifting as you all age, the lobed outlines
morphing in your fingers. You begin to wonder if the frame
is as fixed as you had thought, and then even your vantage
point begins to feel unstable—or mine does, anyway. Sometimes the puzzle itself seems to be floating away from me.

I told myself it wasn't a midlife crisis, because that's
when you want to be someone else. I believed that I'd gotten through most of that kind of flailing about before my
life began in earnest; nearly forty when I married Amanda,
I was forty-three when Addison and Walker were born. I
told myself I was just having a midlife slump. A crisis is
vivid (the crimson Ferrari, the pink slip); a slump is simply
a gray mass of days. I'd wake pinned by cares at 5:00 A.M., the
hour of remorse: overdue tax payments; overdue museum-
permission forms; an overdue article; Roth IRA regret.
Sometimes I'd pad into the kids' room to admire them as
they slept—Addison clutching a stuffed penguin, Walker
hand to heart, pledging allegiance.

When you're young, the past is just steps behind you,
tracks in the snow. By plopping each boot in its previous
imprint, you can backtrack to inhabit twenty-one, fourteen,
six, four. Gradually, imperceptibly, the snow melts and the
track muddies and a silent severing occurs. Twenty-one is
somewhere to the rear, but the way back is a bog and darkness is drawing on.

Still, I came to believe I was a better father nearly every
day, a better writer, more myself. (There was a huge aster-
isk attached to all this positive self-talk, but I tried not to

think about it.) Then, the moment competence seemed at hand, decline heaved into view. Attempting to outrun it was ludicrous, of course. I sometimes think of the elderly Tolstoy fleeing his wife and his doctors, fleeing for his life, and getting as far as the waiting room of a train station at Astapovo, where death was waiting. Then I think, *Tolstoy? Bit of a reach.*

Mom saw herself as overmatched but valiant; her favorite self-descriptive adjective was "desperate." Even her accounts of picking up dry cleaning fizzed with drama. She'd declare, "I crept out at the crack of dawn" or "I scurried home," verbs suited to a small animal in a children's book. When she was weighing what her grandchildren should call her, a top candidate was "Mousehead"—Day's nickname for her short, gray, post-chemo hairstyle. Our kids, who never got to meet her, call her "Foffie."

A poet in her youth and later a painter, Mom was above all an artist of domestic life. She made exquisite meals in the Julia Child manner, then hid any leftover date-and-nut bars or almond cake under her bed, to be rationed out as she saw fit. She arranged each room of her house for maximum effect, and it remains a minefield of memory-bombs: her still lifes, needlepoint pillows, peekaboo nooks concealing televisions and stepladders, silver *objets* deployed around the living room like actors in an Albee play.

Though Day spends most of his time in the open kitchen and dining room, his custody of it extends only to the contents of the freezer. Mom dominates the area still with her hexagonal window plan, pegboard wall, Marimekko pot holders, and shelf of skeptically annotated cookbooks.

Ringed in by her bequests, Day couldn't have escaped to a retirement community if he'd wanted to, which he adamantly did not.

Some houses are garrulous, their interior life voluble on the lawn (the busted TV, the worn-out davenport). Mom's, an old stucco gatehouse largely hidden from the road, was private, cozy, and exacting. Pungent with woodsmoke and Chanel No. 5, her lair demanded that visitors toe the mark. The blue armchair Day had chosen to answer Timmie and me from, for instance, was the one Mom positioned me in, in 1997, to ask me about my then-dismal romantic prospects. In her journal at the time, she registered "sadness about Tad and his slight attention to me," adding "Tad is rude at times" and "Tad's not getting married. Not my fault. My life shouldn't be spoiled by his choices."

Acknowledging that she hadn't always been the most obliging mother, she told me she wanted to fix things between us. "It seems easier now to raise children, because they have those carriers where you go into a museum and the child goes with you," she said, referring to BabyBjörns. "I can imagine, as a grandmother, wanting to take a child to a museum. But when I was a child that never happened, so I basically liked to spend time alone." Training her blue eyes on mine, that tractor beam, she said, "Day and I tried very hard to pass on less loneliness than we got."

That struck me as true, and admirable, and insufficient. "It was a worthy *goal*," I said, staring her down. She was right: I could be sort of an asshole.

I asked Day, "Is there anything you've always wanted to ask us, or tell us?"

"No." That familiar asperity, when he felt or anticipated a challenge.

Timmie cleared her throat. "Is there anything you wish had been different between you and the three of us?"

"I never thought of that," he said. His cheeks began to burn. "And now that I do, I don't like the idea. So the answer is no."

"And what about between you and Mom?" Timmie continued.

"Well, that was an intimate affair. Forty-three years."

"So there's a lot there," she said, encouragingly. "Is there anything you wish had been different between the two of you?" He'd been stunned, after Mom died, to discover that while she'd saved every Lands' End catalogue since 1963, most of his cards and letters to her had vanished. He searched the seven nooks where she answered mail and had a locksmith open her three locked chests: all were empty. His fear, I'd later learn, was that she had burned his correspondence "the year she wrote that she did not love me anymore, and told me not to answer." They each impressed on us that life was not a potluck but a formal dinner with French menus. You could so easily choose wrong.

After a silence, Timmie asked, "You still with us?"

"I'd like some ice cream now."

"We're almost through."

I looked doubtfully at our list. "Was there a specific time—a minute, an hour, a week—when you felt acute happiness?"

"No."

"What is your proudest accomplishment?"

"Running Swarthmore for nine years."

Timmie asked, "What was the lowest moment in your life?"

"Sometime in Buffalo when I feared that I wasn't going anywhere." The hand flick: move on.

"Do you believe in God?"

"Yes."

I said, "Is there one religion that seems closest to your idea of God?"

"Buddhistic Presbyterianism." When he was eight, he'd had an epiphany in Sunday School and yearned for God to test him as He had tested Abraham, but at that age you don't have sons to sacrifice. Unsentimental about most holidays, he loved giving Valentines to Mom and Timmie and later to his daughters-in-law. In 1982, he sent me one, writing, "I deny the thought that it may be un-American or unmanly for a father to send a Valentine to his son." It was a postcard of a mournful seventeenth-century painting of Christ, chosen, he said, "because the face of Jesus is dark, robust, enduring."

Day was delighted when anyone likened his pendant earlobes to the Buddha's, and he relished the Eastern saying "Before enlightenment: chop wood, draw water. After enlightenment: chop wood, draw water." He loved chopping wood. Drawing water, and other household tasks, not so much. After Mom died, I had to tell him the facts of life about the dryer—that it had a lint screen, for instance.

I observed, "Buddhists and Presbyterians have very different ideas about why we're here and where we're going."

"That's true," he said with satisfaction, as if I'd made a rookie mistake. "And in the truth of that resides my comfort."

*　　*　　*

When I was doing physical therapy recently for a frozen shoulder, I glimpsed my face in the mirror and my whole body stiffened. I'd never perceived a deep resemblance to my father in photos, but my bleached wince was exactly Day's in a painting Mom made of him after he had prostate surgery at fifty-seven: stripped and scoured, ashen in his flannel bathrobe. The painting revealed what Day sought to keep hidden—and what I had inherited, to my dismay: a hatred of indignity. *And my increasingly noisy sneezes!* I thought. Day's sneezes echo like rifle fire in a box canyon. *And the way we bang our heads!* Day was always reeling away from low doorways and glaring back. *And my sweet tooth!* When Walker and Addison see me angling toward the cookie jar, they cry, "Daddy, no!"

A few months before that weekend, I was visiting Day and one morning a new health aide arrived for her shift, came in through the front door (everyone uses the back), walked upstairs, knocked on my door, and pushed it open. I started up from the sheets, bewildered by this stranger in a pink smock. "I'm Angela, and I'm here to take care of you," she said, advancing with a placatory air.

"No!" I said. "No, you want my father." I pointed to the far end of the house. She studied me, uncertain.

When Day began to fail, it felt like he was tugging me with him. My sense that we're tethered on a conveyor belt had given rise to two absurd and contradictory beliefs. One is that when he goes over the edge, I'll be pulled over, too. The other is that if I can dig my heels in, somehow, I can stop the belt.

"What are your feelings about death?" I asked.

"I have no feelings," Day said. "Certainly, no fear."

"Have you come to any determination of the purpose or meaning of life?" Timmie said.

"No."

"Is there anything important you would still like to do?" I asked.

"Sure." His voice was softer, less decided.

Timmie inquired, "And what might that be?" His eyes fluttered. "A nap, maybe?"

He laughed. "I am thinking about it. I'm just not getting anywhere."

He lived largely in his youth now, writing about his mother and father. But then he'd always maintained a shallow depth of field as a historian and spiritual supplicant, telescoping right past us in the foreground. When he went abroad he'd prepare at least six words of courtesy in the local language, seeking in exchange only the secret of how to escape himself, of how to live. Or at least a little consolation. Succor would come from strangers, if from anywhere.

"Well, those are our questions," I said. "Is there anything else we should have asked you about?" That's how I usually end interviews. The person I'm talking with rarely raises a new topic, but the question rounds the session off. And sometimes—

"Oh, yes," Day said, brightening. There was always that undertow beneath the swell of his logic—a riptide of eagerness. The child playing hide-and-seek who peeps over a sofa, hoping to be seen. "You should have asked me about my sex life."

"What do you want to say about it?" I asked, cautiously.

"That it was not promiscuous, but it was imaginative."

Timmie and I exchanged another look: *yuck*. "Anything else on that? Or do you want to leave it there?"

"I'd like to leave it there."

"Perfect. Any other topics?"

"My sporting life. Soccer and squash." He played varsity soccer and squash at Williams, and kept them up.

"Those are things that made you happy?" Timmie said.

"Yes."

"What was the high point of your soccer life?" I asked.

"Playing in that league in the Philippines. With practices and games, I played almost every day."

"And of your squash?"

"Being number two in the USA at age seventy-five."

"You almost won the Nationals, right?" In that tournament, veteran players age into a new division every five years. I began playing the Nationals myself a few years ago.

"I had the winning shot on my racquet," he said, wistfully. His right arm carved the air, redirecting the ball.

When I was three, we moved to Ithaca, New York, for a year while Day studied Bahasa, the predominant Indonesian language, at Cornell. It's the first house I remember: small, cool, strafed by morning light. One evening, Mom and Day had a cocktail party in the backyard: pigs in a blanket and Herb Alpert on the stereo. I clambered out of bed and saw Day whoop as a champagne cork shot into the night. I padded through the crowd and reached up as he filled the plastic flutes. "Elizabeth!" he called, and jerked his head at Mom, who led me back inside.

The next morning, I found corks all over the lawn, like shotgun casings. Inside, at the Danish modern desk where he spent his days, Day was writing, "I wake this morning with a duty to my own happiness: to record it. Contentment makes a poor diary entry. Happy is the man that has no autobiography."

Journalists and historians share a belief that the truth is hidden, and likely to dismay. When a childhood friend got married in Vermont, years ago, I admired the reverend's broad, raspy Boston voice. The rasp suggested roast lamb and crisp February mornings and Subarus scattering snow, an assured and ceremonious way of life. But it was throat cancer.

We always feared that Day's house sheltered secrets greater than the vagrant cupboards and cracked sinks, the toilets that ran merrily away from every plumber who gave chase. But when we had it inspected later, in 2020, it was a shock to discover the wood rot and dangling wires; the uncoupled dryer vent that had furred the soffits with lint; the squirrels in the attic and mice in the basement nesting on hidden beds of vermiculite.

The biggest secret lay in the twenty steel file cabinets in his study. Day never discussed his files; they were simply tools in his workshop, arranged as other men arrange their drills and power saws. It turned out, when I began to go through them, that his cabinets preserved memorabilia from every country he'd ever visited, letters of introduction, letters of recommendation, letters of appreciation, letters of protest, lengthy memoranda to his doctor about his latest symptoms, and notes and annotations on clippings about an enormous profusion of topics, including "Aging Artists," "Burma," "Cosmology (Higgs Boson etc.)," "Cyber-anarchy and Other Anarchies," "Jefferson and Slavery," "Neurotheology," and "Prostate, etc., for Fictional Purposes"—his compendious effort across six decades to fathom the universe and his place within it.

Intermingled were folders of his private thoughts: "Journals 1975–76," "Ruminations," "Celebrations," "Verses," "Brevities 1993–96," "Assizes," and scores more. His mind had poured compulsively onto torn-out pocket calendar pages, index cards, legal pads, hotel stationery, envelopes, Post-it notes, and restaurant menus, covering them with snatches of dinner-party conversation as well as with aphorisms, poems, fears, regrets, and prayers. These confessions were a red thread of fervor woven into the snowy vestments of his rational mind.

Like many public men, Day bloomed at the lectern. But he bloomed even more abundantly in private, writing of the delight he took in his glowing fresh-cut lawn and in clear cool sunrises and in the fragrant steam rising from a cup of Lapsang souchong tea—and of his shame at failing to live up to his image as a public man. He was haunted by his dreams: of thwarted or copious urination, of humiliation, of futile effort, and erotic reveries of all kinds—even about Melanie, an old girlfriend of mine, which gave me a shock. His nightmares mortified him; he lived in dread of his unbridled imagination. One night in 1984, he started up from bed to record: "Somehow, after great denial, and without guilt, I find myself near climax in an auto-erotic state, and I am able, to my surprise, and a delight almost philosophic, to get my cock in my mouth. As the expected climax nears, however, I see through the bars of the footboard of the bed the Chairman of the Philadelphia Saving Fund Society peering at me, unblinking, unspeaking."

It wasn't even slightly funny to him, because he hated embarrassment. He hated how ruddy his ears and cheeks got, hated that his face was a heat map of chagrin. He kept the radioactivity at bay through these makeshift journals, treating them as a kind of collider where super-cold electromagnets would channel the flood of energy far belowground, so that he alone could measure the muffled explosions.

On the drive home, as we navigated the nervy merges near West Orange, I told Amanda we'd gone about it wrong. Timmie and I should have talked to him ten years earlier, or asked him to write us a letter to be opened after his death. Something, somehow, to shoulder the door open. But what?

As we hit the seagull-ridden landfill of Staten Island, the traffic increased. We inched across the Verrazzano, along the BQE, and over the speed bumps of Brooklyn Heights. Finally home, we scampered up the staircase, with its threadbare crimson carpeting, to the enameled blue-and-white "No. 2" on the nail.

Amanda reminded everyone to unpack before doing *anything* else—as always, a beat late. Walker and Addison had run to the front window to repossess our apartment. Scrunching their noses against the glass, their breath already clouding the view, they looked back on the way we had come.

Standing behind them, I thought about how, when we'd left Day's house, he leaned into me in the driveway, his whiskers delicate as superfine sandpaper, and murmured, "I adored having you." My heart had cricketed. "Adored" was a Mom verb; I'd never heard him use it. It reminded me of the way he was long ago—or maybe just of the way I'd always hoped he'd be.

Borderlands

THE HEADWATERS of your parents' love are hard to imagine. All you see is the river tumbling by, the river that will carry you downstream to your own marriage, whose origins will in turn mystify your children. I have enormous nostalgia for the honeymoon snapshots of Mom and Day in the stretchy ski pants they wore to drive through the Canadian snow to Mont-Tremblant; that interlude before I was born is all brimming cocktails and boundless possibility. Picturing it is like passing a house on a winter night ablaze with light, shining so your heart jumps. Only it's someone else's house, and you have a long journey ahead.

My parents labored to mark that way for us. But their divergent approaches to almost everything made it a boulevard and forced us to choose: local route, or express lane? Day was late; Mom was early. Day balanced his checkbook to the penny; Mom was often a thousand dollars overdrawn. Day believed in Pepto-Bismol and ciprofloxacin; Mom in bee pollen and vitamin C. Day took trips in stride; Mom hated flying, and always looked for a baby onboard, believing that a newborn would ward off a crash. When friends sent her a singing telegram on her birthday, Day wrote that "a badly sung telegram was delivered by a slightly fruity bearded young man in a red lamé suit"; Mom wrote that it was "Quite scary!" He tried to master his anxieties; she to express them.

Day wore dark tweed jackets and sturdy leather boots and looked calm and reliable. He identified with Walter Pidgeon, the actor best known for playing opposite Greer Garson in eight films. A craggy, husbandly, somewhat inattentive presence, Pidgeon could get away with gazing vaguely at his wife while delivering lines like "You're really quite a beautiful woman, aren't you?"

Mom could never hide her feelings—her festivity and alarm. She had a half dozen best friends who loved her, which often entailed coaxing and cajoling her. When we went to Europe, in 1979, her entries in our family journal included "Checked out Mme Josette's hotel: looks *much* quieter than ours," "Money woes: no cash," and "Terrible cold all day long." Yet she'd amaze us with her loon call, cupping her hands and blowing into the crack between her thumbs as she waggled her fingers to create a thrilling tremolo.

In 2000, she wrote me, "Day has signed on for a 10-day conference/tour in Israel in March, about truth as seen by Sufis, practitioners of Zen, Jungians, you name it: all his favorite topics. I am going along as the Idiot Wife"—she drew a dingbat face. Her correspondence was speckled with smiley and frowny faces and chancy spelling: "fowl weather" conjured up a rain—or reign—of chickens; "enthousiasm" encompassed millennial excitements.

(Years later, Addison announced, "Here's how *I* spell it: e-n-t-h-o-u-s-i-a-s-t-i-c!")

As she caught up, at length, with someone on the phone, Mom would note the keywords on a scrap of paper ("mono, boa constrictor, amethyst, carabao—caribou?") so as not to omit any morsels when she circulated the news. In 1980, she wrote me a prismatic letter about how they'd gone to New York, "Day on college business, me for fun," and a friend from Wainscott, on Long Island, where her family had a summer house, "whisked me to La Grenouille for lunch. The room is filled with fresh flowers + the light bulbs have been dipped in some scarlet pink glaze so that all who enter look ravishingly healthy + glowy: apparently the same technique used to be used on the Orient Express, + Garbo had the famous interior designer Billy Baldwin steal one of their silk lampshades so he could reproduce the glaze throughout her boudoir!!" She refracted life into bright bars of color.

I always hoped some woman would save me as Aslan the lion saved Eustace in C. S. Lewis's *The Chronicles of Narnia.* Eustace, a pompous nuisance, had such dragon-ish thoughts that he was transformed into a dragon. After Eustace reformed, Aslan ripped off his scales, layer after painful layer, to free the boy trapped beneath. I wanted to skip the reform part and just have someone peel off my exoskeleton so everything could pour in: cartwheeling kids, music from a smoky bar, petrichor after a spring rain.

When I was single, my route to that realm was naps. Surfacing from the deep-sea napthysphere, I wouldn't know whose bedroom I was in, or any of the journalistic basics: the who, what, where, when, why, and how. Groggily reassembling my personality, I hoped I'd fit together better this time.

I yearned to somehow reinhabit the happiest hours of my childhood, when I was six and mantled in snow at my grandparents' farm in Woodstock, Vermont. My flying saucer creases my snowsuit as I trundle it up the hill, my boots squeaking in the powder. At the top of the tractor track, I hand the saucer to Day, then slide down the hill on my butt to the frozen pond and turn, knees bent like an infielder and mittens outstretched, to catch the saucer when he sends it coasting down. It's a game we've created, fooling around. After a while, Day tows the saucer uphill for me, and then, when I grow very tired, he tows the saucer uphill with me on it. After dinner, he gives me a badge he's scissored from his legal pad: "Gold Medal For Saucer Catching and Rescuing."

Mom would have cut the shambles short after one immaculate run. In 1963, when I was eight months old, she wrote to a psychiatrist named Marie Nyswander, who'd published a popular book about frigidity, to request a consultation. "I must talk to someone," she said. "The birth of our son, and all the circumstances attending it, have brought matters to a head." She hadn't felt ready for a child, "fearing what it would do to the marriage"; it was Day who had wanted one. And, as she later told me, "You were always spitting up and going through your whole wardrobe." As a toddler, I ate Comet, deadly nightshade, and one of her birth-control pills. When I wasn't having my stomach pumped, I was asking questions she found "incessant": " 'If Jesus is one of God's helpers, and Santa is one of God's helpers, and we killed Jesus, why didn't we kill Santa?,' etc. etc. etc. etc."

Mom's notes from her sessions with Dr. Nyswander, under the heading of Day's "pampering himself when I can't," included:

> breaking things (chair), T.V. set scraped on window sill
> writing in books—plundering, destroying
> wanting ice cream
> using lots of cream + sugar
> letting me make vacation arrangements, get the Xmas tree
>
> = men are brutes

She held me for photos, but not much otherwise. I was often banished to the sunporch of our house in Buffalo so she could make tea and have some privacy in the kitchen. The air in the darkened living room between us crackled like a force field. I can still feel the sun beating through the mullioned windows and the earthy smell of the window-boxed geraniums hitting my throat like an anesthetic, as if the room were an operating theater, the patient spot-lit on the table but no one attending. My father at work, immersed in history. My mother at her desk, immersed in postpartum perfections.

I moped, hoping the radiant beams of my sulking would draw her. The infrared star of Bethlehem. When I was three, she observed in her notebook, "Tad drew pictures of family. Momma was either very small + pointed or not included at all." Yet I was studying her, trying to absorb her protocols. She noted, "Tad announced from the privacy of his room that he was gathering nuts. When I went in, he had stacked all his blocks beautifully and originally on the shelf. I exclaimed with pleasure (he hates to clean up his room, at least as far as the blocks go). Later he told his father, 'It wasn't just a neatering.' "

I kept getting sick. Mom wrote, "In the middle of a week of fever, Tad took a pail in one hand, my hand in the other, and said, with a sweet wistfulness: 'Now we're going to go looking for joy.' " The doctors took my tonsils out. When I awoke to the sunrise burning up my hospital bed, Mom was by my side. She'd been there all night. My throat ached so that I couldn't speak, but when we got home, she brought a tray to my room that held a black-eyed Susan in a tiny vase and a big bowl of vanilla ice cream. If you wanted your own way she would never acquiesce. But when you were helpless, she was perfect.

Me and Mom and my grandparents' dog,
Heather, in Woodstock.

The month of my recuperation, Day wrote, in an e. e. cum-
mings vein, "Yesterday they were in the garden when I
came home. She put on the sprinkler and let the boy play
tag with the water, running to and away from its pattern,
and finally wet, go again and again to the center, put hand
against the hard spray near the source, and laughing run
away. She had been weeding: put a wreath of vagrant vine
around his brow and tied it; and so he barefoot cavorted,
skin wet, green leaves flopping in his eyes, a stumbling
drunken Bacchus of a boy." His note recalled to me the
oscillating sprinkler, and the game of running in through
vapor rainbows to smother the nozzles, the jets pulsing on
my palms. But I never saw him watching from the window.

The next paragraph of Day's entry was about an old
girlfriend, now married and living out west. He'd just had
lunch with her on a research trip; the tab on this file was
"A Journal of Two Loves." From the coast, he'd written to
Mom: "Dear you are to me and very dear: my sandpiper
and my porpoise, bird and fish of my heart, the only one
who can go wherever I go and do whatever I do." But privately he'd noted, "The effort of willing only one series
of thoughts—of wife and child and vows—seems to fal-
ter. I am a romanticist, craving elusive, precarious love. I
wish, but cannot have, the distant woman; I have, and fear
to lose, the one nearby . . . I am in pain." He was reading too much Henry Miller and Simone Weil: license, then
the lash. "There is a province, a whole rebellious province of myself, that I must yield to the Kingdom. In the
government of self this is where the civil war begins: this
province of sensate desire must be absorbed, its outlawry
suppressed."

That evening, out of the blue, Mom assured him, "You're a good man. You would always be faithful when the chips were down."

One night five years ago, as I tucked Addison in, she asked, "Why are we here, Daddy? Are we just a story told by other beings in some other universe? What is the meaning of it all?" She was staring up far beyond the top bunk, where Walker lay rag-dolled. Kids' tests are always pop quizzes. I said that even if she was never able to answer those ultimate questions she'd find other sources of meaning in her life, as I have in her and Walker. She pooched up for a good-night kiss, only semi-satisfied. Fair enough.

An hour later, as Amanda was arranging her pillows, she said, "I saw a male sea horse give birth on Twitter today." She described the whole thing—how the sea horse bucked and writhed, turned white in agony, then finally ejaculated eighteen hundred babies. She popped over for a kiss and fell fast asleep. The curator of a popular Instagram feed, Amanda loves stray beauties and babies of any kind. She was entranced by a podcast about an octopus that spent years guarding her eggs against an army of crabs, and last summer, when we arrived in Wainscott, she placed a clay urn sideways in the peegee hydrangea in the backyard for robins or cardinals to use as a nest. I watched from the second-story window as she hopefully checked the urn, day after day: any bird was welcome!

We were introduced in 2000 by a mutual friend at *The New York Times*, where Amanda was a food writer. She liked my voice on the phone: "Deep and strong with a bit of a crackle," she said later. Her warm brown eyes and fine-boned face reminded me of Audrey Hepburn. On our third date she slipped her hand into mine as I walked her home in a misty rain, and then we kissed under a streetlamp haloed with vapor, suddenly onstage in a movie musical as the orchestra was striking up. She took easy things like a kiss so seriously, and hard things, such as her evocative writing, so lightly. Her fingers flew over the keys with no more ceremony than if she were ironing a napkin: a spritz of steam, then a few firm strokes to erase any wrinkles.

From reading a few of my pieces, Amanda had some-how formed an impression of me before we met: I was tall and lanky and wore dark-framed glasses (true); I had a slim wife with long brown hair and two children (true soon enough); and I drove a Volvo station wagon (not at all true). One issue that troubled Amanda from the beginning was that we couldn't afford a car. Another issue was that I could be, well, me. A few months in, she called me late at night: after a work trip she'd flown for hours to get back to me, and she was terrified of flying. I said I was too sleepy to come over, and she cried, "Passionless fool!" which almost got me out the door, but alas not quite.

Still, we had such momentum. Our bedroom contains a photo of us drinking champagne at a wedding in Spain. My knees are bent and my shoulders tilted, as if I'm about to sweep her into a dip; Amanda, laughing at something out of the frame, is giddy and beautiful and open to whatever's next. She was so alert to possibility, to fun. You can tell how attracted we were to each other—there's an almost audible powerline hum.

She began writing a column for the *Times Magazine* about dating me, plus recipes, and then she turned it into a book, *Cooking for Mr. Latte*. She was wryly amused about my foodie failings—the way I'd say, "Time to tie on the feed bag," for instance—and wildly overgenerous about everything else. She saw me as smart and funny and as a feminist and equal partner. She hadn't noticed my slummier aspects, because I hadn't let her. Sensing an invisible barrier, she'd cry, "I'll take you down!" before leaping on me to bear me to the ground. These assaults made me laugh— but my instinct remained that we should keep doing our separate things, only together.

In our wedding ceremony, at the Wainscott house the following year, we itemized three things we loved about each other. One of Amanda's was "I love that you can open a bottle of champagne without flinching and are the first to fill others' glasses," and one of mine was "I love your passionate conviction that each day is incomplete without a bowl of ice cream." She said, "I'm marrying you, Tad, because you put a spring in my step, because you make me want to be as generous as you are, because I can trust you to know me. And because our relationship has made me happier than I ever knew I could be." I said, "I am marrying you, Amanda, among many other reasons, because my heart jumps with gladness whenever I see you."

Pier read Raymond Carver's "Late Fragment," a call and response that gave voice to our hopes:

And did you get what
you wanted from this life, even so?
I did.
And what did you want?
To call myself beloved, to feel myself
beloved on the earth.

Then we slipped wedding bands on each other's ring fingers: two lefties in a righty world. The gold coil bulked behind my knuckle, a tight fit. My only piece of jewelry.

As the reception drew on, I began bracing for Day's toast. I knew it would be embarrassing, because I knew it would reveal to everyone that he understood loving your children to mean "full provision for" rather than "full communication with." For years I'd behaved reassuringly—*the whole Dad project is going great!*—so he wouldn't feel sad about having gotten it wrong. And maybe, too, so I wouldn't have to examine the whole son project.

His toast went fine, in the end, because he didn't actually give one. He stood holding a champagne flute, having had a few glasses, and said, "Elizabeth says that I'm really much better at responding to queries than giving speeches. So—are there any questions?" He grinned, bashfully, and everyone laughed.

Amanda and me at our wedding reception, 2002.

We spent the week after the wedding alone at the Wainscott house. One cloudless September afternoon, we ate lobster rolls and drank beer, watching the planes for Europe and North Africa blaze contrails across the sky. All those paths could be ours.

Amanda seemed to promise a world of peasant blouses and lazy lunches at hole-in-the-wall cafés. The tireless work she turned out to be capable of, the throughput of it, astonished me. When her hands fell into her lap and she appeared to be listening to distant music, she was imagining something new and stupendous—a book, a company, a way of life. Seizing her to-do list, she'd start making notes.

After we married, she let slip that when she was four, she demanded her own room, and her older sisters had to share. And her family had zero "No, after *you*!" to them; when her dad grabbed her sister, Rhonda, after she snapped at him for having an affair, she stomped on his foot and broke it. Tom Hesser was a fiery self-made man who sold BMWs and Chevrolets in Scranton using promotions like the Jell-O Jump. When his dealership burned down, early on, he rented a trailer, towed it to the lot, and kept on selling. Every Christmas Eve he delighted and scandalized his children by carrying his shotgun outside to shoot Santa in the ass. Amanda was his treasure: when he died, at fifty-two, after a touch-and-go decade with a heart transplant, she stopped eating for a time and stopped crying altogether. Sorrow was her secret; she almost never wept.

The Poconos, where she grew up, was a hardscrabble world. After all the illness and the flares of temper and the financial reverses (in sixth grade, her grandmother sewed overalls so she'd have clothes for school) and the messy period of the affair (her mother smoking furiously at breakfast, no one explaining anything), Amanda decided *I need something else.* She was drawn to a stable, reliable quality she saw in my parents' relationship, and in me. Just before our wedding, she had a dream that she was alone and afraid in dark waters, and she extended one foot down and felt me—a gentle whale swimming beneath to protect her. That was the best dream anyone's had about me.

Mom recognized Amanda's ambition and her need for sanctuary well before I did. Years later, Day told me that after Amanda and I called them to announce our engagement, Mom turned to him and said, "He's marrying me!"

We took a delayed honeymoon in Asia two years later. Amanda white-knuckled it through each of our nineteen flights, but roamed eagerly wherever we landed. She had always wanted to travel like this, the way I'd grown up doing. We ate a lot of street food—fuchka in Calcutta, mi quang in Hoi An—and she contracted toxoplasmosis, a parasitic infection that forced us to postpone trying to get pregnant. During that ten-month pause, I bought her a teddy bear on a reporting trip in Dubai; it had DUBI lumpily stitched on a rear paw, but bore a confiding expression. She slept with it under her arm, for practice.

After the kids were born, in 2006, all our plans went topsy-turvy. Addie weighed only three and a half pounds, so she remained in the NICU for seventeen days to fatten up. The doctors were reassuring, but *three and a half pounds.* I remember seeing her in an incubator, an hour after she'd arrived with the faintest of cries: her Mahatma

Gandhi face, worried frown, and tiny arm dwarfed by its IV line. When I fed her a few teaspoons of milk, she slurped so gratefully.

I remember that after Amanda pumped her milk, we'd each feed one kid a bottle, then pose them on our knees for a burp-off. Addie usually burped first, but Walker's belch reverberated.

I remember that Addie's first word, at nine months, was "Dada." She uttered it like a blessing the morning after I carried Walker, who had croup, into a steamy shower at 3:00 A.M. A week later, I was proudly telling friends that Addie now said "Dada" all the time and Amanda clarified, "She doesn't *really*, she's just going 'Dadadadadada.'" Addie promptly looked at me and said "Dada!" and Amanda cackled with delight.

I remember that Amanda refused to let the kids default to pizza or mac and cheese; they would eat whatever dish she was testing, be it squab or calamari. They would learn the catechism. "What did you have for dinner?" she'd ask.

"Red beets," Walker would say.

"Red beets and . . . ?"

"Chicken!" Addie would guess.

"That was so not chicken. What was it?"

"Fish!" Walker would cry.

"It *was* fish, that's right!"

"Chicken!" Addie would argue.

"No," Amanda would say, smiling. "It was roasted cod with thyme, salt and pepper, and olive oil."

I remember that just before the kids' second birthday I taught them "boo-boo," and instantly regretted it, because they canvassed my skin for weeks to itemize every freckle,

wrinkle, and scar: "Boo-boo!" So much damage to catalogue. So much to protect them from.

I remember that Walker called morning "the early
times." At night, full of hope, he'd say, "In the early times?
Can we kick the ball?"

But most of their first three years are a blur. I shot endless video with a Handycam, but we had no time to watch
the replay: the twins were ball bearings that rolled off to
lodge themselves under the remotest, tippiest tables and
dressers. By Sunday afternoon, Amanda and I would be
supine on their rug. I began to understand that being a parent means literally giving your kids your life. At least, for a
while—until it's too late for them to give it back.

One of Day's favorite maxims came from Joseph Conrad:
"In the destructive element immerse." He invoked it to
endorse turbulent experience—erupting volcanoes, teeming
poverty—in remote locales. When I was nine, he gave me a
copy of *Black Like Me,* so I could experience what it would be
like to be a white journalist in his late thirties who dyed his
skin to experience being a black man in the 1959 Deep South.

He had no equivalent maxim for turbulent experience
at home. In 2007, Amanda took a photo of Day holding
Walker and Addie in our kitchen. Cradling a onesied twin
in each arm, his button-down shirt the periwinkle blue of
his eyes, he looked keenly amiable. His girlfriend, Mary
French, an energetic art teacher who'd been with him since
Mom died, smiled over his shoulder at the scene. When the
kids began caterwauling, though, Day said, "What a squall-
ing! A squall of children!" A displeasure of grandfathers.
He'd have hated it, two years later, when they built a "fire-

works channel" in our hallway out of strips of bubble wrap
and leaped on it to release every possible explosion. But by
then he'd stopped visiting. He was photophobic, he said, and
when he slept in our living room too much light poured in.

A dependable rule of human affairs is that there's more
fucking going on than you think. To understand Watergate,
follow the money; to understand desire, follow the covert
glances. Still, when I recently discovered a file of Day's
titled "Annals of Carnality 1948–1958," I paused for a minute, considering. Then, of course, I opened it.

It was shocking. It was shocking because it made him
seem passionate and fallible and contradictory and human—
and like a total stranger. He described encounters with
another boy at St. Paul's School: "Stripping naked in the
darkness we took fond measure of each other." The second
time, the boy's room was filled with cigarette smoke. "Perhaps that was exciting to him, breaking a rule of the school,
but the smoke was offensive to me. I immediately took it as
an excuse to report him to the class president for the rule he
had broken, without reflecting at all on the rule I had entered
his room intending to break myself." He wrote that his first
female lover, in college, a woman named Pearl, "said proudly,
'That was my first orgasm,' and then lit a cigarette. Somehow
enraged at this anticlimax of pollution, I slapped her hard
across the cheek. Not having the language or the courage to
explain myself, I left." Sex and smoking and churlishness—
when did Day become Jean-Paul Belmondo?

His mother's second husband, Charlie Kenworthey,
asked Day if he'd like to go out with Charlie's former mis-
tress. Day said sure, but when she began to strip for him,

he cut the evening short. A few years later, he ducked out of a potential threesome with an acrobat friend and the acrobat's wife, who'd started massaging both men as they watched "a bad blue movie." Day put himself in harm's way—then drew back. Though he disdained Zen masochists who rose at 3:00 A.M. to sit under cold waterfalls, he often woke at that hour and turned to God: "Last night, unable to sleep, I called on Jesus, asking for forgiveness for lust of power, carnal lusts, all my worldly preoccupations."

His first Jungian analyst asked him, "Have you ever considered that you might be a sensualist?" and likened him "to the form of lizard with a tongue like a shrimp which lays out the 'bait,' patiently waits, then snaps up its fish prey." His next Jungian, he wrote, told him that "I am an 'erotic seeker.' A description, not a condemnation: 'It keeps you alive in some ways.'" Later in life, he'd begin to wonder if striving to contain his desires within the vows of marriage and the commandments of Christianity might not have been a mistake—a self-betrayal.

He felt sorely divided. Yet he knew that without arrant passions there'd be no need for laws and logic, and he took pleasure in composing aperçus about this elemental tension: "The top layer of hell is reserved for those who do a beautiful thing badly; the bottom layer for those who do a bad thing beautifully." And "Civilization, properly awakened, consists of a simple and intricate two-step: 'Thank you' and 'Forgive me.'" Many of his adages had a folksy vigor reminiscent of *Poor Richard's Almanack*: "The rule of head, belly, and heart for approaching happiness day by day: be clear-headed in all things, a little bit hungry after meals, and ready to express authentic affection at any moment."

Civilization and clarity were his lodestars, and the apho-
rism his sextant.

While I'm the house oracle for grammar, current events,
ancient history, and our bank balance, as well as the geogra-
pher and chauffeur, Amanda is the lawgiver on most other
big questions, from the cost of lamps (not twenty dollars,
it turns out); to the best way to plunge a toilet; to when to
tip, gift, soothe, or praise. Also, naturally, on food. Not long
ago, when I was making our Christmas meal, I called out in
a panic, "There aren't enough cloves to cover the turkey!"
"It's a ham," she explained, gently enough.

Our marriage, like many, is a Venn diagram. In the middle
are the things we like doing jointly: being with Addison and
Walker, lingering over a second cup of coffee, planning and
taking trips, watching *Mystery Science Theater 3000*, watching tennis and playing tennis and competing at everything
from pool to Ping-Pong to the daily crossword. On either
side are the things that I don't expect her to do (wake early,
haul garbage, deposit checks) and that she doesn't expect me
to do (inspect grout, save ribbon, bake cakes).

Naturally, we try to enlist each other in our preferred
passions and chores. I succeeded with beer, which Amanda
now drinks readily. She scored with Halloween, previously
my least favorite holiday. Loving its role play, she sewed and
painted costumes, first for the kids (made up as a ladybug
and a Volkswagen Beetle, they became "two bugs"), and
later for us all. We trick-or-treated as four of the five bor-
oughs of New York City (Staten Island, as usual, getting
overlooked); as aspects of summer vacation; as a sushi dinner. The kids learned that the holiday wasn't about sweets

the first time she weeded out their candy bags—"Too sugary," "Too orangey," "Cheap," "Tastes like wax"—and they stared in shock at the scant remains.

Distressed by my *Mad Men*–era culinary skills and *Dead Poets Society* fashion sense, Amanda encouraged my efforts at the stove and resized my shirts from baggy to sleek. After no more than six or seven years of stout resistance, I began to enjoy both cooking and looking quasi of-this-decade. Still, I could never fold a towel to her satisfaction. I protested that she folded our five varieties of towel (dishcloth, washcloth, bath mat, bath towel, bath sheet) five different ways, and why?

Towels are just a skirmish in the battle of the borderlands. One issue is that she came from a "Pick you up at the airport!" culture, while my family were die-hard "How was your cab ride?"–ers. Another is that I'm a demon for efficiency. I dislike waiting in line at a restaurant or meandering around Whole Foods to see what's new. Amanda often gets her exercise from a fast walk, which strikes me as the worst of both worlds: you're going too fast to enjoy the stroll but not fast enough to work up a real sweat. I will run if I'm chasing a ball or a thief, but otherwise I would rather walk, only not fast and not far. It's not like I drink orange juice from the carton—I'm not an *animal*—but I do hate expending more energy than necessary.

Amanda maintains that many of the activities I deride as tasks are viewed by more life-affirming souls as opportunities for delight and growth. Rather than reflexively cooking one of my four or five go-to dishes, for instance, I could tackle one of those two-day Thomas Keller stew recipes that requires reducing a bushel of carrots to murderously small cubes. We could do it together, and it would be fun! Uh-huh. I argue that by speeding through things I don't relish I can spend more time on those I do. Amanda counters that if I won't join in an activity she enjoys, I'm closing myself off to her. To her, love means never even thinking, *But it's inefficient.*

My parents wrote up life plans every few years so they could embark on more projects, develop more friendships, and wring more from each day. In 1965, when I was two, Mom ran the Junior Group and kept up a grueling dinner party schedule and worried about not having conceived a second child yet—all her friends had at least two—feeling that she needed a new "center of gravity."

Day, meanwhile, envisioned his working life as a tripartite affair, like the U.S. government or the Christian godhead. History, fiction, action. Whichever arena he was laboring in seemed less fruitful than the promise of the others. "A poem," he wrote, "is the child of an instant mated with a constant." But when he sent the small reviews such poems as "Sheba, Why Do You Pretend?" and "Torpor, Wrapped in a Turkish Towel," they boomeranged back. So he turned to his history, a comparative study of Indonesia and the Philippines under Japanese occupation—and then he began to doubt the book's merits, as well as the wisdom of the impending family year in those countries. Should he junk the project, and his profession, and really *do* something with his life? Mom told him, "A cook doesn't commit suicide because the soufflé has fallen."

That May, after a bibulous evening at the city's all-male Pundit Club, which he'd joined for its after-dinner talks, Day wrote,

> As I understand the sense in which they see community I grow depressed: community chest, Republican honesty, Protestant complacence, athletic clubbiness. They care for the well-being of the community. But the community is mortgages, liens, interest rates, property values, the law of contingent remainders, getting children into college, vacations under the sun. They do not feel the community of man: the Black Muslim is a phenomenon to be learned about, watched, controlled by salutary reform. But none of them *feel* like Black Muslims. They are on top, where it's white; have never felt black. They are in power, and power has its own dogmas: they have never been converted to a faith out of miserable yearning and divine ferocity.

He had. Yet he also yearned for the power that he believed his fellow Pundits were squandering.

Family life consoled him, somewhat, for not yet having made a real dent in the world. "I woke the boy and put him in the back of the station wagon with a blanket and pillow; and she climbed back there too with a comforter, and I drove us over the bridge to the Lake's other side and looked at the city, the city's lights, with the eye of a tourist," he wrote, a few days later. "We played the radio: old sentimental tunes, and chattered with the boy, and drowsed. She was droopy as a fern. And said the next day it had been one of

the happiest times in our marriage." In his journals he usually called me "the boy"; people often struck him as ideas
incarnate, as Jesus was. Even allowing for the asymmetry
of parent-child relations, where the parents loom larger in
the child's mind, there wasn't much in his musings about
Timmie, Pier, and me. We usually appeared as subsets of
his own capacities. In 1990, he would write, "One son likes
money; the other, words. My daughter likes massage. I like
money, words, massage, and sacred music." Okay, Zeus.

Writing was his one unfailing balm. "I have benevo-
lence and tenderness in me," he observed, "and no way to
let it out but by writing." Day often regretted the modern
obstacles to a life of contemplation. He might have been
happier as a religious scholar in seventh-century Arabia,
guiding the caliphate, or as a monk in medieval Japan, rak-
ing his pebble garden. He might also have been happier as
Lord Byron—if not quite happy. "Pain is inescapable, and
must be met with suffering," he wrote. "Suffering is raw
and must be transcended with art. Art will be repudiated,
giving one again the opportunity of pain."

The best parenting advice we got, just before Amanda gave
birth, came from a relaxed, amused mom: "Whatever your
kids get excited about, encourage it." She didn't warn us
how many hidden forces conspire to foil this principle—
not least our own strong predilections about what's worth
getting excited about. So we careened as parents will into
another forever war over which of us the children would
take after. Addison has Amanda's fastidiousness, and Walker
has Amanda's interest in design: he'll spend hours online
selecting a bespoke pair of Nikes. But when they were five,

and they were asked their favorite dish on a Food52 podcast, they both said, "Daddy's pasta!" Amanda was understandably chagrined. The problem is that she's always trying new recipes, while barely a week goes by without me making rotelle all'Arrabbiata—a Mario Batali recipe to which I, heroically, add a pound of bacon—so I benefit from the power of habit. Also, it's delicious.

I wanted Addison and Walker to be better versions of me, me 2.0. But I worried that my do-over fantasy would incur resentment and bring about, as in a fairy tale, the opposite of my intention—an even surlier version of me. So I was elated by their resistance. One day when Walker was putting on his sneakers to run through a fountain, I said, "If I were you, I'd wear my Crocs. They'll dry much faster."

"No, you wouldn't," he said calmly, standing up. "You'd do exactly what I'm doing, because you'd be me."

When we arrived in the Philippines, in 1967, Day wrote his father-in-law that "Tad is learning how to ride a bike with trainer wheels. He accompanies all he does with a running string of questions, commentary, and self praise; energy which could just as well be employed in the legs. Well, it's to be expected, I suppose, that one of our children be an intellectual."

Upon leaving the hospital after his visit for eating the Christmas tree ball, he drove me and Mom downtown to see Santa Claus. When Santa's helicopter landed on a platform before a vast, cheering crowd, Day wrote in his journal that "The boy asked, 'Does it say "Santa Claus" on it?' I didn't answer, for it actually said Manila Hotel." Mom and Day both teared up at this equatorial beatitude. Mom said, "I wonder if the Day of Judgement will be as nice?" As Day hoisted me onto his shoulders so I could see better—I dimly recall a glimpse of red velvet—he felt a jostle. Someone had stolen his wallet. "Santa was stomping around the platform," he wrote later, "waving like a retired prizefighter or a confident aspirant for the Senate. I put Tad down and looked in the faces behind me, all gazing at Santa in lovely benediction. The man nearest, a clerklike white-shirted small man, had three children in front of him. Anybody could have done it, E. said, and I said yes. So I just turned back and watched Santa, my tears dry. The mood of faith and fulfillment was gone, and I felt adult again, a man with a career, with responsibilities, with his boy on an outing with a pocket empty of all the identification papers he had so laboriously gathered from the tropical bureaucracy." Longing to lose himself in a yearning throng, he'd again been repulsed.

I was slow to realize it, but Amanda had a comprehensive plan to pull me out of the past. Phase One was promising to take me for better or worse. Phase Two was purging my squat sofas, law-firm-style bookshelves, and storm-door-on-sawhorses desk, and then insisting, despite my miserly objections, that we renovate some troublesome part of our apartment whenever our bank account hit five figures. In the lulls between these derechos, she shunted to storage or the curb a semi-abstract painting of the sea crashing on dark rocks made by Mom's mother, Grandma Tim, and all the rugs I'd brought home from my travels. I greeted each innovation as a trespass, but loved the results. Phase Three was introducing me to the joys of toast tongs, dryer balls, and a Japanese butter spreader.

Whenever the four of us escaped New York in a Zipcar, after a lot of trundling of car seats and Pack 'n Plays and muttering of curses, the radio invariably played the Harry Chapin song "Cat's in the Cradle":

> *My child arrived just the other day*
> *He came to the world in the usual way*
> *But there were planes to catch, and bills to pay*
> *He learned to walk while I was away*

Before kids it had seemed maudlin, but now it made my throat ache. Sometimes I could barely see the road.

The kids loved Harry Chapin Playground in Brooklyn Heights, which they called "Happy Chapin"; the folk singer grew up playing there, just off the Promenade, with its glorious view of Manhattan. They were always asking us to take them to Happy Chapin, a few blocks away, to watch them run through the fountain and push them on the swings. Just for one minute, Dad? One afternoon Walker gutted us when he catalogued our excuses: "I just got home"; "I just showered and I'm all clean"; "Okay, but in ten minutes/half an hour/an hour"; "Weren't you just outside?"; "I have a phone call"; "I finally got settled"; "I'm too tired"; "It's dark out now, sweetie."

Even so, they were bursting to share their discoveries. "Two little monkeys coming to bother you!" Addie would cry as they tumbled into my study. Then she'd say, "If we lived inside a rubber-band ball, we could bounce to school!" Or

Walker would say, "Dad, may I tell you some amazing facts? Did you know a lightning bolt is no wider than a quarter?" When we were watching a Red Sox game on our giant couch, he asked me, "What's your favorite body part?" As I considered, he said, "Mine is my arms, because I get to hug you."

One night I sprawled on the couch with them and we all sang along to George Ezra's "Budapest," the children piping the melismatic "you"s. *But for you, you, I'd lose it all* ... They thrust their balloon heads close to confirm that my eyes were wet: "Why, Daddy, why?" It was the purity of their voices, and of their belief that George Ezra would always matter. They didn't know about one-hit wonders.

In grade school in Buffalo, I'd wait by the door for Day to get home and save me. I'd show him a new penny in my collection—the 1925 S!—or kick a ball with him in the yard. He coached my soccer team, the Panthers, and one evening we drove to Toronto to watch Santos of Brazil play an exhibition. On the way home we discussed Pelé's goal until I fell asleep.

After I lost an election for president of first grade, I sobbed. Day wrote Mom from the Netherlands to observe, "He is truly our son, is he not, with a foolish combustible mixture of ambition and sensitivity?" Responding to her news that a family friend had said that I might be a genius (a notion that's been thoroughly disproved), he added, "This brought strange tears to my eyes and a rush of feeling: what if he really *were* some kind of whatever; well no, God spare me having a genius for a son, and spare him too; and after all, *I* am the only genius in the family."

In second grade, two shaggy little shits held me up at

knifepoint and took my red Schwinn. Day drove me around in his Beetle looking for them. I'd recently been mugged for my library books. Rough town, Buffalo. We could have talked about that—my fear of being bullied forever—but he had a simmering look as he wrenched us around the corners: the vigilante professor who leads the local news. When I was sunny, he was benevolent, but when I was morose, he got angry. Luckily, the little shits were long gone.

Me, Day, and Pier in our jungle gym in Buffalo.

In 2008, six years into our marriage, I gave Amanda the first draft of *Cheerful Money*, my book about growing up a Wasp. She swooped off with it and gave me bright-eyed interim reports. Then, flying home from San Francisco after a work trip that had gone badly, she read chapter six, about my first passion, for Natalie, who "was a shocking lash to all my senses," etc., etc. My intent was to show how idiotic I'd been, and why—I kept pursuing Natalie for nearly a decade, though she had a string of boyfriends and slept with me occasionally only to make wounding remarks as she again withdrew—but I was also proud of my foredoomed ardor. Rosy accounts of two other early loves followed.

Amanda came home crumpled. *The ones you really wanted got away, so you settled for me.* I told her that I truly, deeply loved her, and that she was the only person I'd ever wanted to marry, and that it's easier to portray failure than contentment. That was all true, but I was also trying to placate her and make my escape. Amanda *was* the right woman for me, even when her fierceness alarmed me. But I wasn't sure I was the right man for her—or, really, for anyone. I'd occasionally flirted with other women after our wedding, assuring myself that it was harmless, that nothing would come of it. *It makes me feel better.* It made me feel worse, too, but it made me feel better first.

I rewrote, and we patched things up. But I'd let her down. It felt like Amanda started to seek closeness now through shared duress: "I'm thirsty—are you?" "I have a head-ache—do you?" When she told me how important finan-cial security was to her—constantly hustling, she was now testing recipes for and writing a massive *New York Times* cookbook at night—I coolly declared that we'd probably be just fine. This struck her as unsympathetic and obtuse. We were beginning to realize that she looked ahead, expecting to grow, and I looked back, hoping to maintain.

Unilateral action emerged as a possibility. Amanda had always been entrepreneurial: in seventh grade, dismayed by a charmless hallway by the school cafeteria, she designed a sports mural for the space and enlisted her classmates to paint it. After college, she pitched a women's culinary group and got them to underwrite sending her to cooking school in France and working in restaurants in Italy, Germany, and Switzerland. When she began pumping breast milk for Walker and Addison, she decided there ought to be a better support pillow, and came up with the Swottle. She asked founders for advice and built prototypes; her Swottle had pockets for twin bottles, was stylish and cozy, and addressed an actual problem. Though I loved it, and her for making it, I saw her idea as a potential side hustle, no more.

But Amanda was determined to try something new, to take a big professional swing. In 2008, she quit the *Times Magazine* to launch a start-up. First Seawinkle, a visual timeline of your digital life, which died fast, and then Food52. I admired her moxie, her willingness to take a flyer on a long-shot plan that wouldn't earn her any money for a while—and might well fail entirely. So I'd encouraged her to take the risk. But hadn't the tacit contract been that we'd just be journalists who griped a lot and bumbled along?

Building a company proved a struggle. Amanda didn't take a salary for several years, and we loaned Food52 most of our savings. By 2011, our bank balance had plunged eighty percent. The following year, we had to borrow

$13,000 from Day and $13,000 more from Amanda's mom to pay our bills. It began to feel as if our future hinged on the company. I gained a reputation, among our friends, as the enlightened husband who took care of the kids on the weekends while Amanda worked. This wasn't quite fair—if she'd been the man, no one would have thought twice about our setup—but I didn't go out of my way to correct them. I was at last being seen the way I wanted to see myself: as a long sufferer, a quiet hero.

As our children grew, Walker sought to map the world and pinpoint his place in it: "Which would be faster in a long race: Usain Bolt, or an old, tired donkey? Okay, and how many women, adult women, in America would you say I'm nicer than?" When Addison wasn't alarmed by the randomness of existence, she gloried in it. Trying to filibuster through her bedtime, she asked, "Can I just say one more illogical thing?" Once, as Amanda and I were having a sotto voce quarrel, Addie skimmed into the kitchen wearing a teeny crown: "Bow to the king of all kings!"

"Wouldn't the king of all kings have a bigger crown?" Amanda asked.

"That's why it's funny!"

It was around then that Addie's OCD became apparent. Was the bomb she was afraid of buried within our bickering? I hope not. But Amanda and I began to worry that Addie's perfectionism derived from her fear that our family was so fragile that even a B+ English paper could blow us apart.

At seven, she told us that she wished to be called Addison; she would no longer be diminutized. Walker absorbed that, then forbade us to call him "Froggie" or "Mr. Moo" or "Walkie-Talk": "It's Walker or Walkie. And only Walkie for you guys."

When Addison asked, "What's in an empty cup?" Walker declared, "Nothing."

"Wrong. *Air!* Air is everywhere."

"Except in outer space."

That night, she announced from her bunk, "I'm thinking of nothing," and Walker objected, "Thinking of nothing is actually thinking of something."

A less exhausted parent would have introduced the weak anthropic principle and explained that the only reason we believe the universe contains something is because we're here to perceive it. A moderately resourceful parent would have observed that if the strong anthropic principle is correct—if the universe exists to create us, its observers— that fact could resolve Addison's question about the meaning of life. A stupendous parent would have gotten them a podcast. I called out "Bedtime!"

When I went in to kiss them, a few minutes later, Walker declared from the darkness, "I am Mr. Carbon Dioxide. I am invisible!"

Once they turned ten, Amanda and I tried to ready them for the years ahead by calmly introducing them to the facts of life. Neither of us had gotten any guidance about sex from our parents; Mom handed me a fifties-era gynecological manual and fled.

As we bombinated on about love and relationships and sperm and eggs, Walker slid off his chair to lie on the floor gazing in horror at the ceiling. Addison listened wide-eyed, then darted off to read the book we gave each of them, *It's*

Perfectly Normal: Changing Bodies, Growing Up, Sex, and Sexual Health, which had seemed, in my quick sift, to be admirably matter-of-fact.

Amanda shrewdly left town on a work trip. A few hours later, having read the entire book, Addison raced into the kitchen with questions. "Okay," she said. "Did people in George Washington's time have sex?"

"Yes," I allowed.

"And in Cleopatra's time?"

"Sure. Sex has been popular for quite a while now."

Having lobbed a few softballs to relax me—classic journalistic technique, by the way—she pounced: "So, did you and Mom do the butt one?"

Addison has long maintained the Salingeresque view that childhood is a privileged position. At five, she declared that she wanted to be a seventeen-year-old camp counselor forever. As a tween, she's lost some joy. When I wake her for school, at 6:10 A.M., she protests, "Can I just have this moment?" or "I was growing!" She recently told me she'd be willing to enter a portal to an imaginary world, "but only for fifteen minutes. I've got homework." Yet when Amanda asked her, "Do you want me to teach you how to vacuum?" she declared, "No, my mind is already full of other things!"

A few nights after that exchange, I found Walker in the doorway to the kids' room, wearing a crown of scarlet felt that I'd picked up in Mongolia. Finger to his lips, he commanded silence. He and Addison were playing "Invisible": you close your eyes and feel your way around the room, hoping to tag someone, as the other players tiptoe out of reach. Addison had climbed the ladder and stood on Walker's bunk, eyes shut, clutching the air. Seized by dread, I darted over with my arms out. Then I made them promise never to stand on the top bed with their eyes closed. Invisible—ugh! It's not just the neck-breaking aspect. It's the groping for your family as they laugh and slip away.

As Walker changed into his pj's, he performed his galloping jackass dance, hopping and hooting and slapping his naked butt. He approached the dance as gravely as an orchestral tuba player tackling his solo, so it was hilarious. But it turned out to be his final performance; he'd outgrown it. The following morning, he emerged from a ruminative silence to say, "I'd like to be 99.999 percent a genius, and .001 percent just very smart, so I won't have the burden of being a genius."

"Good plan, Froggie."

When we shared our New Year's resolutions, last December, Walker said, "After dinner, at night, it would be great if we could all do something as a family, instead of everyone separating to work." He began to get teary. "Because I like being with you." So often, providing entails a deprivation. You look up from that work email and they're five years older.

Mom became a much better mother later, after Pier and Timmie came along; Pier was so easy, she always said. As a parent, you learn on the job. She sought me out to atone—and sought me out, and sought me out, and sought me out. *How was soccer practice? What are you reading? Would you like a snack—some lovely cool grapes?* I was charmed by her, and we laughed a lot, and it was all amicable and loving moment to moment, which is where children live, most of the time. But I kept her at a certain remove. *You're too late.* She felt this, and hated it.

When I was seven, Day recorded that "Tad wrote a composition about his mother. She was afraid of it. She forced a smile and asked, 'Is it full of bad things?' He said he didn't want anyone to read it. Going to bed, she worried about it, and next morning, while he was upstairs, she peeked at the composition. It says, 'Her voice is like a moonbeam, her living room is a palace and I love her. She would have been a princess. She is very pretty and she is interested in sports (at least she listens) and I wouldn't want another one.' She leads me out to look at it, and when I've read it, I look at her. Tears start from my eyes, and tears from hers, with a rueful smile at herself." My first big descriptive lie.

Three months after we saw helicopter Santa, Day went to Indonesia to conduct interviews. It was Mom's idea: he was despondent about his research in the Philippines, she wrote her mother, "feeling that there were no surprises to be discovered here, that two years of his life had been wasted." She added that when she suggested the trip "we both knew instantly that it's the only thing that can give him back a sense of his own worth. So, grim as I feel about it, it has to be done. Poor Tad is only just beginning to settle down into the boy he was before August. How he will endure his father's absence I don't know."

In Jakarta, Day felt himself drawn to his fixer, a woman I'll call Siti Z, which is what he called her in a work of history more than thirty years later. A former actress with a forthright manner, Siti Z was at ease in the political world and had "style, intelligence, integrity," he wrote. He embarked on a novel about the triangle that was taking shape in his mind. "Did the fictional impulse draw me toward adultery, or did the adulterous impulse push me toward fiction?" he asked himself. "Hard to say." He prayed that he could transmute his turbulent feelings into limpid prose. "If it's published," he promised himself, "I might work the thing out by 'vertical stories,' going back in my past, rather than 'horizontal stories,' reaching out to other women."

Burning through the onionskin pages of his hotel stationery, he decided that his crisis stemmed from having lacked a role model in his own father. "Time to realize, to make *real* the thought that this is the age when others need *you* as father. So learn that role, that job, that joy, and take pleasure in it. OK, OK, I do, I do." Though he had two sons and Mom was pregnant with Timmie, his thoughts immediately turned to the ultimate progenitor: "Well, then, now: what about 'God the Father'?"

The following night, as he ate a solitary dinner, he was stunned by a revelation: "the powerful sudden appearance in my mind of a crucifix: wooden, blurred in color, weathered in form. My whole being was swallowed in convulsive sobs and the tears streamed down my face into the rice." Buoyed, he believed that he would not have to see a minister "to get the strength to be faithful. This vision will be enough."

Two months later, back in Manila, he added, "BUT IT WAS *NOT* ENOUGH."

*   *   *

When she was seven, Addison wrote a story about us, with beautifully blobby pencil-and-crayon illustrations. I recently found it behind the couch in my study:

> One nite me and Walker lookt out the wendoe at the snow. That was because me and Walker wantid are dad to come home so we cold play in the snow. So wane our dad came home we got owr jacits and glovs on. Than we went out side. Than playd and rote in the snow. It said I Love you mom. Than we rote it agin. Than owr mom came home and we had a snow ball fite. We thro and thro than mom slipd. Than we thro and thro and thro and momay slipd. Than we went in side and were happy.

It's normal that they have different memories than we do, right? It's for the best?

Twist

WHEN WE were young, Day once called Christmas "a wretched carnival." After that, our gift cards for him proclaimed "Merry Wretched Carnival Day!" On Christmas morning, he'd retreat to the bathroom after breakfast and stay there until Mom sent us to beseech him through the door. "Dorie!" she'd call, from the kitchen. "Dorie, honestly!" Only then would he return. He wanted his absence noticed, wanted a search party with helicopters and Boy Scouts and Saint Bernards.

Day's parents, Ted and Jess, bought him every Christmas gift he picked out in the FAO Schwarz catalogue, but they never kissed him or told him they loved him. They reserved their emotional energy for despair when Ted got blackballed from the Pittsburgh Golf Club. They had so wanted to fit in. Heirs to ancient lineages of wound-lickers and grudge-nursers, Ted and Jess thereafter stayed focused, respectively, on boozing and cheating. Amanda says that I resemble Ted, with my humid eyes and long, puzzled forehead.

At ten, Day wrote his mother from camp, "I am very homesick. I don't know where my sugar ration card is. . . . I don't think you gave me the envelope which had the sugar card. . . . Everybody else is happy which makes me feel worse. . . . Please send me (if you have it or if I haven't lost it) the sugar card." His essay "My Father," five years later, reads as unintended satire: "My father is always glad to get home and relax. He reads the paper, drinks a cocktail, and can't be budged. After mother finally gets him into the dining room, he will talk on his favorite subjects, 'Taxes,' or 'What Roosevelt has done to the United States of America.'"

Fired from his brokerage at forty-three, Ted would slowly drink himself to death. When Day and his younger brother, Charles, were at Williams, Ted asked them to meet him in New York, where he announced that his and Jess's marriage was a mockery because "your mother has been laid, relaid, and parlayed by every man in Western Pennsylvania." Then Ted got back on the train and drank all the way to Pittsburgh. Jess, who turned to at least five other men after alcohol made Ted impotent, divorced him and married another cocktail soul—the love of her life, the charming Charlie Kenworthey. After he died of cancer a few years later, she found a genial third husband and took frequent cruises.

When Day got married, he dreaded his father's toast: at Charles's wedding, five years earlier, Ted had slurred out a few disjointed phrases and collapsed into his chair. But at Mom and Day's rehearsal dinner, Ted got so drunk he had to be escorted back to his motel before the speeches began.

Day was determined to break free of that backdrop. He became a historian because no one in his family cared about history, and he specialized in Indonesia and the Philippines because they were about as far as you could go from Pittsburgh without drowning. An avid student, he applied for every prize and fellowship. "Starved of affection," he wrote, "I grew hungry for honor."

At Swarthmore and the Eisenhower Exchange Fellowship, Day excelled at fundraising and liked to call himself a "not-for-profiteer." He washed his hands with warm water beforehand, so as not to offer a cold handshake—Ted always said, "Never give 'em a limp fish!" Day tried not to emulate Ted in other ways, but feared he'd forever have to "endure my father's deprivation and humiliation; that I spoke in his cracked, embarrassed voice; that public contact and decisions that for others were ordinary were crises of confidence for me." Unaccustomed to having to articulate or defend a point of view, he'd failed his grad school orals at Yale because he couldn't frame a coherent reply to "Mr. Friend, what is a peasant?" He taught himself to declaim by going into the woods with his Sunday School Bible and reading Psalm 1 to the larks and squirrels.

Feeling cursed because "I never had a father," Day sought paternal tenderness his whole life. At the end of his first Jungian analysis, in the late seventies, he yearned to conclude the final session by giving his analyst a kiss, a blessing of peace. They fumbled into a brief hug instead. In 1992, he had a convivial meeting with the longtime prime minister of Turkey, Süleyman Demirel. Demirel, seven years his senior, was warmly commanding, and bussed Day on both cheeks when he left. "The kiss lasted days," Day wrote. "The surprise of intimacy. The thought of blessing from power. The thought of his fatherliness."

*   *   *

Mom's mother's family, the festive Robinsons, waved their napkins when they sang and wept at the mention of Abraham Lincoln. Christmas was their crowning occasion: wreaths and ribbon candy, firs and spruces laden with ornaments, and a conga-line-style march into the living room to see whether Santa had come. As you marched, you intoned, "Hayfoot, strawfoot / Belly full of bean soup / January, February, *March!*" the chant that taught Revolutionary War recruits their left foot (tied with hay) from their right (tied with straw).

Mom took the holiday further still. She began with an Advent calendar, then spent the holiday week cooking turkey tetrazzini and ginger duck and baking lace cookies as the New Christy Minstrels harmonized holiday songs on the stereo. She clipped candles to the tree and lit them, with a bucket of water at the ready, before we sang carols. And she convened a Nativity scene on the mantel: papier-mâché animals (a kohl-eyed ox, a suspended goose, a frisky sheep on wheels) keeping watch over a tiny wicker basket which, on Christmas morning, would immaculately conceive a walnut swaddled in cotton batting—the Baby Jesus. She spent weeks mailing presents to dozens of friends, and her own pile was always twice the size of anyone else's. Where Day saw gifts as reparations, Mom saw them as love.

For her, the crux of the holiday came on Christmas Eve, when we'd read Beatrix Potter's *The Tailor of Gloucester* aloud. It was Potter's favorite of her children's stories, and ours. We'd pass Mom's childhood edition of the book hand to hand, tag-teaming a story we knew by heart. An elderly tailor trudges home through the snow, having laid out on his worktable the components of a coat of cherry-colored corded silk that the mayor of Gloucester will wear to his wedding on Christmas Day. The tailor sends his cat, Simpkin, to the store for supplies, including a strand of twisted silk he needs for the final buttonhole. As he warms himself by the fire, beginning to be ill, knocking sounds come from a set of teacups overturned on the counter. *Tip tap, tip tap, tip tap tip!* We'd chorus this doggerel each of the four times it recurred. When the tailor flips the cups, mice that Simpkin had trapped bow or curtsy to him. As the tailor returns to the fire and mutters feverishly about the mayor's coat, the mice listen attentively—then scatter before the cat returns.

We'd tacitly arrange the reading order to ensure that Mom didn't get the last pages, when the tailor, bedridden for several days, totters to his shop on Christmas morning, clutching his skein of cherry-colored twist. There he finds that the mice have sewn his coat together for him, save for the last buttonhole, to which is pinned a scrap of paper saying, in teeny-weeny writing, "NO MORE TWIST." She could never make it through the moment of discovery—"oh joy! the tailor gave a shout"—without bursting into tears.

Mom's Robinsonian inclination to hoopla was shadowed by a Piersonic gloom. Her father, John Pierson, had graduated from Yale with an array of extracurricular achievements and the highest grades in the college's history. He fully expected, once he was of age, to be elected president. Constrained by diffidence, he instead became a UN economist who wrote densely reasoned books about full employment and Zen. Grandpa John could walk into the surf on his hands and make a linen napkin scurry up his arm like a mouse, but he could not appease Timmy Robinson, his beautiful, high-tempered wife. In 1938, he had a break-down and fled the family summerhouse for Manhattan, where he'd remain incommunicado for a year. A few days later, the Great Hurricane of 1938, which killed six hundred people and destroyed more than fifty thousand homes, hit Wainscott head-on. Grandma Tim bundled her two small children into a Buick and tried to escape, only to run into a fifteen-foot storm surge that trapped them in the car all night. A divorce followed.

Mom, then four, mailed her father a drawing of an empty house and wrote, "Daddy John Pierson I Mrs. You" and "O Come Soon." Believing that he'd left because she'd been a disappointment, Mom developed an enduring fear of catastrophe that she sought to allay with charms and rituals and piles of casualty insurance. Day told her that she had "an unusual capacity for dread." In 1967, he privately noted that their childhood devastations dovetailed: "E. and me, a blessed marriage: she gets a Daddy who won't cut and run; I get a Mommy who won't cheat on the side."

In February 1968, after Day had spent a couple of weeks in Jakarta, he wrote Mom, "Goodness, I wish you were here: it would save me from a lot of boredom, vagrant desire, loneliness, uncertainty." Three weeks later, preparing to meet her in Bangkok at the end of his trip, he wrote, "I think about Tad. I am going to go on writing him even after I stop writing you. I think Tad should get mail when we are away."

That night, he climbed the trellis of the house where Siti Z lived and tapped on her window. When he left, several hours later, he had to climb over the gate at his hotel—he was breaking curfew, among other rules. Siti Z was the lover of Day's best friend in Indonesia, and before he married, Day had gotten involved with the wife of an older cousin he admired. Surprisingly, for someone so disposed to self-accusation, he never seemed to reflect on his need for rivalrous conquest.

When Day's research concluded, a few days later, Siti Z asked him to marry her. She had money of her own, she assured him, and she wouldn't be a burden to him in America. All she asked was to be allowed to visit her lands in Minangkabau once a year, and to be buried there. He reminded her that he was taken. She proposed again a few days later, and he explained again. Then, feeling riven, he boarded the plane.

Before they married, Mom had told him, "If you're ever unfaithful to me, I don't want to hear about it." But as soon as she arrived in Bangkok, he confessed: "In Jakarta I fell in love." They somehow made it through the silent sightseeing at Angkor Wat, the untouched meals. He wrote, "The most terrible moral agony I've ever endured: barely able to sleep, to wake in the morning weeping, our faces like stone, frozen in pain." He later marked Mom's sexual withdrawal from that day: "I never stopped asking E—*imploring*—forgiveness after my affair. But she never gave it. Verbally or—so far as I can see—emotionally." Believing that he'd involuntarily emulated his mother, he feared that Jess had ruined him. In 1984, he would write, "In my own laughter I hear the voice of my mother's lovers."

Back in the Philippines, Mom asked him, "Do you think there can be a great marriage if there has once been a little departure from it?" He said yes. He told Siti Z about this exchange when he wrote her. He wrote her a second letter a few days later, but never sent it. Perhaps it was too definitive: "I don't want to marry out of my own culture," he said. "I inquire into other cultures as a flight from the construction of the culture of my childhood. I solve the problem of my childhood by communicating across a culture gap; the more so if it is to communicate love; all the more so if that love is returned. But finally, what is the most perfect communication? The most complete? The mutual expression of love by two who share the same culture, society, religion, and values. All else is research."

In his journal, reckoning with his decision, he wrote, "I married E. because I knew how to suffer criticism, both explicit and implicit. Face this thought: that to some degree you desire suffering." After we returned to Buffalo, Mom wrote her brother that "it's been a strange, difficult year for us. We learned a lot, but about ourselves rather than about Asia." In her notebook she observed, cryptically, "Tad winter 1968–1969 'sprained heart.' "

When Addie was three, she appropriated Amanda's DUBI teddy bear for her menagerie. When we tried to winnow Addie's mound of plush, she under strenuous protest got rid of her two scratchiest animals, leaving just ninety-six. When she read the final installment of the Harry Potter series, her face bright with wonder and worry, the bear was clutched under one arm. She explained that he had wizardly gifts: "His superpower is, he snots on you."

"That's not much of a superpower," I said.

"His snot is huge!"

Our kids loved the rabbits in *Watership Down* so much—feisty Bigwig; runty, prophetic Fiver—that I read it to them again a year later. The book's perspective is enchantingly leporine; the rabbits venerate the mythical El-ahrairah, a trickster rabbit much concerned with stealing lettuce, and they don't die, they just "stop running."

Around that time, Amanda and I began ventriloquizing some of Addison's and Walker's animals. Amanda did Bertrand, a languorous, self-important UglyDoll who served as my assistant and claimed credit for all of my accomplishments. I did Bernard, a patchy, one-eyed bear from Amanda's childhood who was deeply if haphazardly affectionate—he called the children "Waker" and "Anderson"—and who showed his affection by farting in your face.

I was fluent in this kind of dumb show, having grown up in a family where naked expressions of feeling were felt to be injurious. Beginning when Mom was small, Grandpa John and she would exchange drawings and photos of baby pandas, otters, elephants, and mice, and Mom conveyed love to us by stuffed animal. Timmie got Duckie, a duck whose floppy neck Mom resewed at least ten times; Pier got a blue blanket called Blankie; and I got a yellow-and-pink one called Quiltie, which I adored down to its batting. It was so soothing to tuck its knotty corner between my fingers and lay my cheek on its ragged train. Day retired Quiltie when I was twelve: "You're too old for that now." As a child, he was forbidden to suck his thumb—he had to wear aluminum mittens until the danger had passed—and his only blanket or stuffed animal was a handkerchief.

*   *   *

When I was eight, Day took me to Pittsburgh for the weekend, and we visited my ninety-three-year-old great-grandmother, Lillian Friend. Blind and deaf and almost bald, she slurped prune juice through a straw. *Sprawk!* I had never seen anyone so old and feeble.

He told me that on the day Lillian became the first woman in Pennsylvania to get a driver's license, she ran her Model T into a tree. This makes her sound madcap, which she spectacularly was not. At her Sunday lunches for Day and his parents, an inviolate meal of roast chicken, mashed potatoes, creamed onions, and ice cream, Lillian's conversation consisted of spirit-quashing remarks such as "Curiosity killed the cat." If anyone asked your news, you'd say "Nothing to report." Toward the end of her life, Grandma Jess would write Day that marrying into the Friend family meant embracing tedium: "They were all always *very* polite and non-committal, as though they were really strangers to each other. No problems of any kind were ever discussed." To her credit, she ended the letter, "And, I guess perhaps for the first time, I am writing that I love you very much. I wish I had been able to say that many years ago, but I'm learning. Ma."

That night, at dinner with Lillian's only child, Grandpa Ted, and Ted's second wife, Eugenia, I finished off my grudging scoop of vanilla ice cream and licked the spoon. Eugenia, a world-historic harpy, addressed my father, "I cannot *believe* that you would raise a grandson of *mine* to *lick* his spoon!" I fled the table in tears; Eugenia retired in a huff; Ted gave me a set of James Fenimore Cooper in tipsy apology; we left at dawn.

Day at his Swarthmore inauguration, 1973.

When I was ten, Day took the Swarthmore job. We'd been happy in Buffalo, or happyish, anyway, but his ambition needed running room. The president's house was a field-stone manor with so Escher-like a profusion of staircases— six in all—that on the day we moved in, Timmie, who was four, got disoriented at the top of one and lay down and cried. When I took Addison and Walker by the house a few years ago, their squinty expressions helped me see it fresh: it was imposing, in the way of armories and rhinoceroses. But Lord was it ugly.

The night of Day's inauguration, Grandpa Ted drunkenly vomited all over the downstairs bathroom. What upset Day more was that his father never congratulated him on attaining the presidency. Ted died three years later, the healing words unsaid. Within weeks of taking office, Day was beset by students protesting the Vietnam War (which he'd publicly opposed since 1965), captious faculty, and a treacherous board. By Christmas, he developed an ulcer and was gulping Gelusil. His new three-piece suits couldn't disguise the twenty pounds he'd gained, the protective padding.

When Day got home, at 6:00 P.M., I'd ask him to hit fly balls to me. Occasionally, he'd shuck his jacket and belt fungoes for twenty minutes. But usually he'd say, "I have a phone call," and head to his study with a cup of tea, closing the door. If you tried to get his attention, he'd eventually smile and cock his head, but his mind was elsewhere. In his journals, he now wrestled not with mastering himself, but with the murky gambits of others. In place of crisp aphorisms, he composed baroque dialectics. A few years in, he wrote, "I knew, in my narcissism, that I saw myself as Saint Sebastian, and loved the role. That I would will a suffering, so long as it were significant, and neither accidental nor degrading. I suppose I have found it in a college presidency."

Constantly simmering, he often boiled over. Once, talking to Eugenia, he began waving the phone at his crotch. Mom hated when he closed his eyes as he listened to her— his theatrical forbearance—and hated even more when he'd chop his right hand sideways to cut off her appeals, final as the headman's ax. He wrote, "My wife: If I did not cherish her integrity and depend on her loyalty; if I did not value her intelligence and efficiency; if I did not admire her ethics, judgment and taste; and if I did not thrive on her cooking, I couldn't stand her."

Day's truculence made all three of us side with Mom. Her asks were reasonable—more family time, more comforts—and she was so forlorn it was clear she was the wounded party. Yet she forbade us from following their lead: "No arguing!" And no one seemed to want to hear that I found being the president's son, in a small college

town, a misery. I'd slink off to my room to listen to songs
like "Bad Company" and "Dream On" because they suggested a world beyond Swarthmore, a world full of drugs
and outlawry and skintight pants—a world that was not
actually in my future, but that gave me hope for some very
different future, somewhere else.

When Day went on research or fundraising trips, Mom would
slip a stuffed bear named Malta into his suitcase. Five inches
high and claret colored, the bear had black stitchwork fea-
tures that gave it the sagacious look of a consigliere. He was
intended as a dual-purpose charm. First, he would keep Day
safe; second, Day would open his bag in Bucharest or Kuala
Lumpur, be charmed, and remember to come home, to leave
off drinking toasted almonds in hotel bars. Ten years after his
fateful trip to Jakarta, he flirted with a restaurant hostess at a
conference in Cambridge, Massachusetts. "I wish I could tell
a lovely young woman what love I feel, unconditional and
undemanding, giving it as a gift and passing by with no more
possessiveness than I feel for an old man sitting on a bench
in the sun." He suggested a drink; she demurred. "I felt then
and after as if there were a hot coil in my mind: I could see
it burning, a dull glow like an electrical range on low."

Meanwhile, we got a 120-pound Newfoundland named
Molly. She shed wads of hair and developed a battery of
ailments, from dandruff to hip dysplasia to cardiomyopathy,
but she doted on us. When Mom was profiled in the college
magazine, she said, "I always wanted to have a lion, and
Molly is what I have instead. She has a small brain but a
large heart, and gives us lots of love. She seems to be more
expensive, more time-consuming, and to require more

medical attention than any of the children, but I adore her because she is totally uncritical."

After Molly died, Day told Mom, "I want to be your dog for a while."

"Oh, Dorie," she said. "Who would train you?"

She promptly got a tiny Tibetan spaniel. Sam would bite his toy teddy bear and shake his head, bullyragging it until it flew over his shoulder, leaving him mystified. If Molly was the child Mom secretly wanted, Sam was the baby. Nearly half of the photographs she took after that were of Sam.

Mom's dreams during this period were easily parsed: she struggled up slopes, or was barred by chain-link fences, or found herself having sex with "a man who looked like John Updike." One morning, she recalled that she'd dreamed that "I was being anesthetized in order to deliver a baby. While asleep, I said, 'I want a divorce.' When I woke up, the nurse told me what I'd said. I laughed +, making light of it, said, 'Doesn't everyone say things like that when they're out?' 'No,' she said."

In 1977, after four years of gilded misery, Day wrote Mom a letter of complaint. Her devastating letter of reply suggested that the job had destroyed him—and them:

You have disciplined yourself not to give an opinion. No bumper stickers, no voting or even registering to vote for several years, no Christmas cards to college people we simply like—I can understand all of these as political expedients, but I can see that they also begin to rob the identity of all its specifics. In place of that person who had preferences, appetites, the urge to scratch in public, is erected consciously, brick by brick, another person, a President: one who, forgetting childhood hesitancy, speaks easily and playfully to alumni groups, one who answers the phone with hearty good cheer, knowing it's the chairman of the board, even though the call may be breaking up the one evening that week he has with the family. One recognizes of course the need to be fluid, positive, strong, the one who sets the tone, and one acknowledges that some of the time one even feels that way. But there is also an enormous effort required of self-abnegation as well as what might seem to be its opposite but is actually related: image-making or self-aggrandizement. My question is, after all of that, where can Dorie Friend be found? . . .

Is this why we have such terrible fights?

Is it because you're struggling to preserve your very self and I'm struggling not to be your yes-man, nor your executive secretary, nor your nurse—but your equal partner and wife? . . .

You asked in your letter: "What are we married for (now)?" Well, one thing I'd suggest is that we're married for *fun*. How much fun are you getting out of our marriage? I, for one, am not getting enough.

I believe we must try doing couples therapy. As with surgery and house renovation, things might look worse at first, but I have faith that they would eventually be much, much better. Please let's try.

They began seeing a therapist.

Mom and Day in Swarthmore, late 1970s.

Day fought about Swarthmore's ethos with its major donor, Eugene Lang, who would leave three buildings adorned with his name. There were secret board votes, turncoat allies, broken vows. Day's correspondence with the board— letters that declared "I must say" and "I cannot suppress a few observations" and "I cannot end without being bold enough to note"—burned with a sense not only of mistreatment, but of lifelong underappreciation.

The money won. Lang, desirous of an honorary degree from his alma mater, resigned from the board so he could accept one without breaking board rules, then returned with sweeping powers as its chairman. Lang offered Day an honorary degree of his own as a parting gift, but he refused the sop. At his last commencement, Day announced that he'd prevailed on another alumnus, the founder of Publishers Clearing House, to bequeath the college his residual fortune.

"That was a Parthian shot," Lang murmured, surprising Day with the erudition of his reference to the ancient horsemen who'd pretend to retreat and then pivot to fire a hail of arrows. Day began writing a roman à clef about the struggle, and confided to his journals that "two or three novels may be needed to work out the anger/defeat by Lang."

A decade ago, answering a questionnaire, Day said of this period, "I knew better than to be a slave to my job (at penalty of dying of a heart attack as a predecessor had done), but my children often felt my emotional absence nonetheless. In trying to avoid my father's failures, I may have condemned myself to some empty successes."

In college, I read about researchers who tried to induce depression in baby monkeys by replacing their mothers with, as they blandly put it, "cloth surrogate mothers who could become monsters":

> The first of these monsters was a cloth monkey mother who, upon schedule or demand, would eject high-pressure compressed air. It would blow the animal's skin practically off its body. What did the baby monkey do? It simply clung tighter and tighter to the mother, because a frightened infant clings to its mother at all costs. We did not achieve any psychopathology.
>
> However, we did not give up. We built another surrogate monster mother that would rock so violently that the baby's head and teeth would rattle. All the baby did was cling tighter and tighter to the surrogate. The third monster we built had an embedded wire frame within its body which would spring

forward and eject the infant from its ventral surface. The infant would subsequently pick itself off
the floor, wait for the frame to return into the cloth
body, and then cling again to the surrogate. Finally,
we built our porcupine mother. On command, this
mother would eject sharp brass spikes over all of
the ventral surface of its body. Although the infants
were distressed by these pointed rebuffs, they simply
waited until the spikes receded and then returned
and clung to the mother.

First, what the fuck with that "research"? Second, my
mother was no monster—you'd have liked her. But I identified strongly with those baby monkeys. I couldn't stop
thinking about them; I'd feel a jet of air in my eyes and
black vertigo as I fell away. The feeling was so intrusive that
I stuffed it into the memory hole, where it wouldn't trouble
me anymore.

Now I wonder if, given time, the monkeys would have
eventually retreated to the corners of their cages. Because
that's what I did. I retreated, with many a backward look—
but I took the compressed-air hose with me. "I'm afraid I
left you alone a good deal when you were young," Mom
said to me once, regretfully. Brightening, she added, "But
the result is that you learned to read very early, and now
you're a writer!"

Day spent his first post-Swarthmore year on a fellowship in
Washington, DC. One day, when he needed change for the
bus in Alexandria, Virginia, a black woman gave him some.
That night, he wrote:

And then she asked "You a child of God?"

"I *hope* I am!" I said, and my eyes stung with the ecstasy of unsought protection.

"*I'm* a child of God," she said. "I think you is, *too*. You look like one."

I reached for her as the line surged toward the open bus door and touched her on the shoulder. Our eyes met, two clumsy deputies of a dispersed posse from heaven.

Yet he had a one-night stand while he was living there, and blew up at Mom in a Washington restaurant because she couldn't cover the tab—and because it became clear that she hadn't been putting five hundred dollars a month into their savings account, as they had planned. When she said, "There just isn't anything left over!" he cried, "It's your job to make sure there is!"

Having seen his family squander its wealth, Day was vigilant about expenditure. On one hand-drawn spreadsheet he handed Mom, he noted in red ink that their annual savings rate had decreased from negative 32 percent to negative 39 percent. "I won't try to do budgeting with you," he concluded, "because you have resisted, ignored, and/or breached every budget I proposed." He finally insisted that they keep their money in separate accounts.

For her part, Mom believed that Day was drinking too much. She put it to him: after repudiating his father's habits his whole life, did he really want to succumb now? He did not. Nor did he want to bend to her will. In 1985, he wrote:

I had three glasses of kir at dinner. Then, after dinner, sitting by the fire with E., poured myself three quarters of an inch of sherry.

She looked at me over her far-sighter's glasses.

"Are you disapproving?" I asked.

"No, just wondering."

"Wondering what?"

"Wondering whether that's the best thing to consume after all the kir you had."

"Well, what would you suggest I consume before going to bed?"

She looked into the fire, at the dog, then over her glasses at me. "Toothpaste, perhaps?"

When I traveled around the world for a year, in 1988, I opened my backpack in Honolulu and found that Mom had somehow smuggled Malta into it. When she was about to start her chemotherapy, in 1995, I gave her a Care Bear. It wore a hospital gown and had a gauze bandage attached to its paw. Day wrote me, "Your Teddy Bear made Mom cry in the sweetest way. Every time I go into the dining room, she is sitting on the couch clutching it, or holding it on her knee for conversation."

In 2002, Mom sent me a photo of a baby polar bear curled up on its mother's back on an ice floe. Alluding to her tradition with Grandpa John, who had died six months earlier, she said, "When I saw the enclosed, I wanted to send it to him. But since that is no longer possible, I'm sending it to you instead. With much love, Mom."

*   *   *

In Mom's individual therapy, after the marriage counseling, she discovered that Christmas was actually something of a wretched carnival. "Christmas is a compensation for other, missed love," she noted, after one session. "I should either give presents or not give presents based on what I want to do, not expecting a response. As long as I don't take control of my life (instead I am under the control of Dorie, of Christmas), I can continue to be a neurotic child."

Yet Day was equally in her thrall. In a sketch for a potential novel, he wrote, "He saw doorsteps, bootstraps, tea cannisters, everything, through her appraising eyes. She was a connoisseur of the ordinary and collector of the unique. Everything that fell under her eye was known, almost carnally, at once. . . . The house became a kind of gallery of their marriage. Except that he wasn't in it. 'He can't sit still,' she said, explaining, to a friend, why there was no portrait of her husband in the sweet arcade of arrested things. 'I *can* sit still,' he replied. 'Actually, I am good at stillness.' "

She finally painted Day in 1990, after his surgery for prostate cancer: the flannel-bathrobe painting in which I saw our resemblance. He acknowledged its power: "There was a universal quality of convalescence in it." But he felt troubled by it, too—felt she had waited to paint him at his weakest. The following year, he wrote, "Only after my radical prostatectomy (when I was back at work, but totally impotent) did she say, in a peculiar way that could only evoke the affair"—with Siti Z—" 'I forgive you. But don't do it again.' " When he asked whether she wanted him to take an erectile dysfunction drug so they could resume having sex, she repeatedly declined to answer. "I conclude that the level of psychological antagonism she feels for me is (1) deep (2) quietly vengeful."

To make sure of his equipment, Day slept with a Korean-American I'll call Cho. Years later, in his journals, he would recall that "less than a year after her marriage, she said to me, 'I want to be intimate with you.' That, I felt, was too tender a sentiment to deny. So we fulfilled it in the Plaza Hotel, NYC, during a visit of mine on business." Tender!

Mom always longed for a house she could make her own, transform as Le Corbusier did Chandigarh or Robert Moses did the Bronx. The house in Buffalo was too small and the one in Swarthmore belonged to the college. In 1989, they looked at a two-hundred-year-old gardener's cottage set on the corner of two acres in Villanova. She had hoped for an airier, more modern platform, but Day loved the property's pond and its arboretum of trees—apple, fir, dogwood, Norway and Siberian spruce. So Mom set out to make a charmless shanty shine. She conceived of eleven major projects and lined them up like landing craft off Normandy. She bulldozed three bedrooms to create a master suite, opened up pass-throughs and secret cubbyholes, and carved out a cozy new kitchen, backsplashed with blue-and-white Portuguese tile.

Day cherished a crumbling stone wall that enclosed a bed of pachysandra by the house; its garland of wandering vines reminded him of the temple of Ta Prohm at Angkor Wat. Mom had the wall rebuilt and made tidy, then lopped a mulberry tree he admired so she could set the wall off with two new wooden decks. When she proposed felling a one-hundred-year-old silver maple by the dining room windows, for reasons of light and air and safety, he erupted: he'd been drawn to the property by the way the maple's branches fanned protectively over the roof. He wrote from Cape Town to say, "I would no sooner think of cutting it down than I would think of cutting off a finger." Retreating, for the moment, she insisted that its branches be knit together with steel cables. On blustery days she'd dart from window to window to peer up at the tossing canopy, conspicuously alarmed.

As Walker grew, his body caught up to his huge head, grounding it like guy ropes on a Macy's balloon. But he still took in much more than he let out, so his sixth-grade application essay was a revelation:

> Hello, my name is Walker Friend, and I have a few things I would like you to know about me. I am a very shy and sensitive person and any hurtful comment (unless I know it is a joke) makes me feel embarrassed and sad. Sometimes I even cry.
>
> I want to become a professional soccer player when I grow up, so I practice every day in my room (ball skills, juggling, and passing).
>
> I enjoy math, because it is fun deciding on a strategy for solving the problem and then being able to tell my answer and feeling sort of proud of myself. It feels like wrapping myself in a soft blanket.

Another survivor, sheltering in place.

Later that year, he produced a PowerPoint titled "Miniature Schnauzers. The Perfect Dog." We'd boarded friends' dogs, but Amanda and I had strong reservations about getting one. The dog would be alone a lot; we live on the second floor so we don't have a yard; and kids never pull their caretaking weight. Walker met our concerns with facts and links: miniature schnauzers can be alone for hours; they can use pee pads; here's the skinny on feeding, walking, and kenneling. "Since it is only 17 dollars a walk for Brooklyn Bark and maybe even cheaper for other companies I really don't consider this a major problem," he wrote. "Also since your lonely and mature children are growing up and soon won't need a babysitter you will be saving a lot more money, a little of which you can transfer into your lovable dog's exercise." And if we didn't care for miniature schnauzers? "Well that's mean," he noted, but seven other homebody species would work equally well. He promised to do all the feeding and walking and to take on extra chores to relieve us of every conceivable stress. "This is my dream so please at least think about it and give it a chance." It was an entirely disarming presentation. We said we'd consider the idea, hoping he'd grow out of it.

That October, Amanda transformed herself into a rice roll for our family-as-sushi Halloween costume by wreathing herself in white socks stuffed with cotton. Addison used black and red felt-tips to give an extra rice grain a pursy countenance: voilà, Ricey. When I went through security at the airport the next day, before flying to Los Angeles, I discovered that Amanda had hidden Ricey in my coat pocket. Once home, I slipped it into the outer compartment of her suitcase. It's gone back and forth a dozen times since: open a seldom-used drawer or put on an old boot and there's Ricey.

I have no idea where it is now, which means it's probably somewhere in my possession. Only Amanda can't remember where it is, either.

When I read Mom's and Day's recollections of these years, I felt like the best friend in a rom-com. Yes, they had issues; yes, each maintained a locked room, Bluebeard-style; yes, she was a domestic sensualist and he was a nomadic sophist. But they had a similar quality of mind, a lancing acuity, and they needed each other. I kept wanting to cook up a scheme to force them to meet at the airport. Yet even in the worst of it, Mom's notes to Day were headlined "My own true love," and she dreamed that she and Day were "tied for fifth place in the world's best marriages." Such tolerance of conflict is a vital component of love, and of civilization.

On Mom's birthday in 1995, the day that Day resigned from EEF to be beside her as she battled breast cancer, he wrote her:

> *Together with you*
> *I stand,*
> *Like the two jars*
> *Of olive oil*
> *Bathed in light.*

He was referring to Mom's practice of decanting her olive oil into twin cobalt flasks—and surely alluding to Rilke's famous dictum that love "consists in this: that two solitudes protect and border and greet each other." That credo is either a generous dispensation for human frailty or a poetic acknowledgment of failure. It's worth remembering that Rilke spent most of his terrible marriage miles from his wife.

After Mom died, the hardest part of the following Christmas was making our way through *The Tailor of Gloucester.* Then Scott, who'd gotten married to Timmie three months earlier, read the tailor's musings about whether he'd been wise to set the mice free—"Alack, I am undone, for I have no more twist!"—not in the voice of a frail old man, but of a swashbuckling pirate. "A-*lack*!" instantly became our tag for Scott. Welcome to the family!

Just before Christmas in 2006, *The New Yorker* published my recollections of Mom. I'd begun to write about how you could grasp her emotional history from her house, particularly once you saw the eleven photos of Grandpa John in her dressing room, but it grew into a larger portrait of her warmth and wit as well as her inconsolability. I had asked Day to look the piece over before it was published. His only reservation was about my account of how, when I was unable to sleep on the night Mom died, holding Amanda's hand at 3:00 A.M., I had found myself reflecting on *The Tailor of Gloucester:* "I was almost able to soothe myself by thinking of Grandpa John as the tailor, absent from his shop only because he was sick and frail, and Mom as a faithful brown mouse, sewing busily in the dark."

"I understand this, and *appreciate* it," Day wrote in the margin. "But what would Freud say of seeking consolation in a children's tale? Why not seek out Boethius, *The Consolations of Philosophy,* for a stoic view? Or the Christian story as seen by a great anti-Nazi modern like Bonhoeffer or Barth? The emotional dynamics of engagement at such a level seem far more fertile to me than a needle stuck in the groove of Beatrix Potter."

During our visit that Christmas, Timmie found three copies of *The Tailor of Gloucester* in a hidden presents drawer. They were surely intended as gifts for each of us once we all had children to read them to—which, now that Timmie was pregnant, was about to be the case. Mom was making her closing argument.

We keep an eye on Walker and Addison with an app called Life360. It was comforting, when they were nine or ten, to see their icons cruising down Hicks Street at 4:30 P.M. as the school bus arrived. In a minute, sneakers would patter up the stairs, a key would scrape in the lock, and they'd spill in, tossing off their backpacks.

There's not yet an app that pinpoints their maturing perspectives. The other night, when Addison was bemoaning the frizzy state of her hair, Amanda observed that you can take your worst feature and make it your trademark. "Like Rod Stewart with *his* hair. Or Paloma Picasso, Picasso's daughter, who had a big nose, but who accentuated it and was known as one of the most beautiful women in the world." I made a face. "What?"

"How do you accentuate a nose?"

"She did, by being proud of it."

"Also, was she that beautiful?"

"My point is—"

"I agree with your larger point, I'm just saying—"

"Oh my God, stop it!" Walker said. "You're always arguing and it's so boring!" Addison sighed dramatically and drew a heart in the air between us.

Amanda and I looked over, surprised. "This isn't an argument," I said. "It's a pointless disagreement." Stony faces; appeal denied.

When Walker's friend Zenebe came for a sleepover, Walker allowed, in his postmortem, that we had mostly stayed out of sight. But in the morning, I had made them scrambled eggs while wearing a T-shirt and *boxer shorts*. "Boxer shorts" became the kids' first "Billy Grassie." They'd begun to occupy a parallel-universe facsimile of our apartment. It has the same dimensions, but, like bats or bees, they apprehend it on wavelengths invisible to us.

After Day recovered from pneumonia, in 2008, Mary French showed him Mom's house from new vantages. He wrote:

> *Upstairs she leads me*
> *to my sons' old bedroom,*
> *to my daughter's sunny view of the pond,*
> *All the way up to my wife's studio,*
> *her paints and unwashed brushes.*
> *This is all mine, borrowed from heaven.*

But he gradually disbanded the Christmas circus: no candles, no ornaments, and finally no tree. He redid the house's north wall in drab fieldstone, installed plastic bins in his study to hold his overflow books, and stopped shining his shoes. He built two bedrooms above the garage, so all eleven of us could visit at once, but the new wing was as charmless as a barracks. He was rebutting Mom when she could no longer refute him.

A few Christmases ago, I went into Day's bedroom to say good night and found him tucked up in bed. As I closed his shutters, I said, "The dogwood is really tossing in all this wind."

"I saw it from my desk earlier," he said, his voice softening. Mom had specified the precise spot for his desk, so he could oversee both his tea table near the window and his favorite dogwood beyond. Everything was framed to delight. "I think of her every time I look down the lawn."

The following morning, the huge silver maple fell. Fortunately, it toppled south, not north, smashing the fence across the lawn instead of all of us. It was hard to say who'd been proven correct.

Bombardment

WHEN I was a boy in Buffalo, Day taught me squash. We entered the frosty court by a low hatchway and waved our wooden racquets in stately arcs, ceremonious as polar explorers chiseling out an ice cave. He'd tap the ball to me for a bit, then uncoil and smash a hard forehand, the ball skimming low along the side wall like a mouse racing for its hole. His game was about power.

When I was eight he introduced me to Mohibullah Khan, a mustachioed Pakistani who rose to #2 in the world, at a tournament cocktail party at the Tennis & Squash Club. Khan was in town to beat up on the locals.

"Mohibullah is a first-rate player," Day said, elaborating the syllables of "Mo-hi-bull-*ah*." "Watch everything he does."

"No, no," Khan said, smiling down at me. "It's so cold I'm just trying to get off the court. Come to Pakistan and see how the game is really played."

"I've been," Day said, grinning. And they were off talking about Islamabad.

American squash was a douchey, prep school affair, but Day didn't perceive it that way. He never saw himself as privileged. In the late eighties, he had dinner with Philadelphians who were descended from eighteenth-century Tories, a set still so loyal to Britain that they rose only for toasts to the Queen. Rankled by their royalism, he remarked that his Swedish ancestors came to America in 1648—a textbook snub. Yet he preserved a sense of himself as an outsider, even a sort of rube. His childhood had been so deprived of affection that he took no comfort from its entitlements.

To Day, squash was a field of battle. In his novel, *Family Laundry*, the narrator casts the court as a stage where character is gradually revealed at top speed: "I, forever searching for heroes—or was it fathers?—would . . . command muscle, bone, and nerve; smashing, slicing, dropping the little black hardrubber ball where no opponent could reach it. I would win at this four-dimensional contest of territory and ricochet, this quick, calculating, gladiatorial game." After Day lost Buffalo's B-level final by one point, in 1965, he sent his father a photo of himself shining with sweat, and wrote, "I have an open blister on the ball of my foot, an aching knee, an undiagnosed girdle of pain around my middle. But I did my best (not my most skillful, but my most valiant), so it doesn't hurt that way, inside."

Puberty blessed me late; I only caught up at sixteen, and by then I felt I'd missed it. One day in eighth grade, I slunk out of school after last bell and saw the burnouts, Owen and Pat and Lucy and Sue and Adam and Dave, passing an apple-pipe bong and making out as "Smokin' in the Boy's Room" throbbed on a transistor radio. It was like watching an orgy.

When I got home, I must have muttered something plaintive, because I remember Mom exclaiming, "Oh, darling, you're going to be a late bloomer! And that's just fine—in fact, it's the best thing to be, because you have to develop your character. I was a late bloomer, too!" Seeing my doubtful expression, she went on, "And the kids who are popular now? They're going to end up working in *gas stations!*"

Unexpectedly, she turned out to be right. Maybe not about the gas stations, exactly, but about the value of watching the early birds: it became my m.o. in school, college, work, even marriage. I'd scope the drill, study it, hone it. Amanda likes to say, "You're a chipper-awayer. You're a tortoise. But you win in the end!"

Squash intrigued me when all I could do was plonk the ball and gape at the resulting physics. After college, I started playing a couple of times a week for exercise—and got hooked once I realized how roomy a small court could be. You greyhound into the corner to retrieve a ball caroming at a hundred miles an hour, send your opponent on the longest possible journey in return, then lunge into the far corner, where he's sent your shot, and so on—and on, and on, and on, for an hour or more. Squash looks like tennis at triple speed and feels like heroin without the needles and the vomiting afterward, except when you vomit afterward. The game, above a certain level of skill, is played at a lunatic extremity of effort.

I applied myself and gradually got pretty decent: a cagey

lefty with a deceptive forehand boast, a shot spanked into the side wall that glances obliquely off the front wall just above the tin, squash's version of a net. The default serve is a lob, but Day had taught me to hit a hard serve—to attack from the outset—and that was a weapon, too. In my thirties, I won the Harvard Club tournament a few times and began to think of myself as a squash player. I had grasped not just the game's rules (games are to eleven points, win by two, and a match is best of five games) and its strategy and protocols (you try to hold the center of the court, known as the T, while allowing your opponent a path to the ball; if you get in his way, it's a "let," and you play the point over) but also its animating potential.

My squash friendships are mostly squash-specific: we play, postmortem a bit, then part. But they're stamped by the pleasure of jamming together, of collaborating on a jubilant rag of hissing strings, percussive splats, sneaker squeaks, and winded grunts. Squash provided me with fellowship and exercise and an occasion for magical thinking—for believing, say, that I played better after a haircut because I was more aerodynamic. Better still, it exalted me. All of life's challenges were compressed, for a time, into a box.

I always thought that in a fire the first thing I'd grab would be my journals, where I'd made so many small deposits into the bank of self. In my initial entry, in college, I promised myself "attention to studies, daily conditioning, and squash two or three times a week." Throughout my twenties I exhorted myself to greater discipline, clarity, exercise. I wrote headlong entries after midnight: I would learn

French and Italian. Massage. Photography. Candor. Yet I
complained every time the clocks shifted ahead (the lost
hour of sleep) or back (the lost late light). Change always
struck me as an undoing.

My childhood was gone. But the sensations adulthood
was supposed to supply—the woodsmoke nights and doorway
kisses, the slow warming of cool skin—had not replaced it.
After college, I moved to New York, where I was stunned
by the city's subterranean engines. How was it possible for
water and gas and electricity to navigate all that underground snakework and flow into my $175-a-month bolt hole?
Determined not to betray my innocence, or to make more
than the customary number of mistakes, I took notes: so
this dark coffer is a parlor apartment. So this darker coffer is a dance club. So this blast of hot wet garbage is a
Manhattan summer. So this rumor about "the Bushkin
Munchkin" is office gossip. So this—working late on something urgent and trivial, ordering takeout so you can work
later still, and trying to convince yourself, as you empty the
greasy container, that there's glamour in spending down
your strength—is how you rise. And before long, like every
aspirant who posts an unrefundable bond to make those discoveries, I felt like I owned the place.

The tangible form of the city's promise was a hookup
with someone I barely knew; relationships were for the los-
ers in Kansas City. Without ever discussing sex, Day had
somehow smuggled his sensibility down to me, an heirloom
in a chamois pouch. One morning I woke in a strange bed
with a cat on my face, allergic both to the cat and, I immediately realized, its owner. On my way out, I glanced into
the bedroom of her roommate, who was engaged to a friend

of mine. The squared bolster pillows and the silver-framed portraits of her and her fiancé similarly squared felt like an augury of where sex could lead if I wasn't careful. My walk of shame became a jog.

My favorite bygone world is Patrick O'Brian's twenty-novel series, set during the Napoleonic Wars, about the British naval captain Jack Aubrey and his ship's surgeon, Stephen Maturin, who's also a British secret agent. Each man scintillates with life—Aubrey hearty and energetic, Maturin dour but wildly romantic. Yet O'Brian's theme is the ravages of age. As the years pass, Aubrey's and Maturin's hopes succumb to personal and professional disappointment, and they become inseparable from their roles: the domineering captain and the mistrustful spy. Each keenly suffers this loss of pliancy and verve but feels helpless to reverse it.

At a certain point your daydreams stop. The internal narrator who's so voluble when you're young ("Two outs, bottom of the ninth, and Tad Friend steps to the plate . . .") and who murmurs on underneath your adult endeavors ("The magazine was desperate for an April cover story, and Tad Friend *stepped up!*") gradually becomes inaudible. One day, as you're listening to your cable company's hold music, the Walter Mitty in you tiptoes out for good. Your days and your dreams, now separated, ask for privacy at this difficult time. Then your days begin seeing someone new: your memories.

When I turned fifty, it was the chimes at midnight. Squash had begun to slip away, and I felt compelled to wrench it back—to see how much better at it I could still get. To recover a bit of my Mitty. Or, rather, as I'd be seeking to improve while my body was rapidly disimproving, to see if I could learn how to cut my losses. Like all sports except golf and bowling, squash is a young man's game. Tournament draws are rife with dudes who bound on-court, their earbuds leaking Imagine Dragons, eager to go far too fast for far too long. I do better with impulsive teenagers, workaday women pros, and anyone who has a mortgage.

My goal was to crack the top ten of the over-fifties, nationwide. And my window felt small. Twentysome-things had begun to look right past me, and I found myself envying them their suppleness, their idiot bliss. I consoled myself that I was still slim, still energetic after three mac-chiatos, and that by candlelight in a restaurant bathroom I looked fortyish. Forty-five, tops. (I looked fifty.)

Unfortunately, squash itself was deepening my rut. After a match, my Achilles tendons felt like hawsers on a rusty barge, and as I clomped back to the office I'd get passed by map-consulting tourists. Despite buying analgesics by the tub, often as not I'd bolt upright at 4:00 A.M., an hour before my scheduled 5:00 A.M. remorse, with a searing calf cramp. Laboring woozily not to wake Amanda, I'd winch my calf over the side of the bed and stand to relieve the spasm. During this process, I more than once got tangled in the sheets and pinwheeled to the floor. So there were some issues.

I don't remember exactly when I beat Day for the first time, but I was in my early twenties and he was in his early fif-ties, and he seemed more stricken for himself than pleased for me. At fifty, he had vowed to attain a "national ranking in top 20," and begun keeping a training notebook with the subject line "Attempt to build endurance, speed, and technique in sprint and run." He even noted the conditions on the track: "temp ~ 85, low humidity, light wind." There followed a meticulous accounting of push-ups pressed, sit-ups crunched, matches won and lost, and lessons learned ("knee bend!").

His daydreams began to vanish in Swarthmore, but his nightmares there featured menacing dwarves and scenes in which we children were vivid at last, but as collateral damage. "I see my son Tad in a confrontation with a young man his own age. In their struggle a gun goes off: I see the bullet hole through the heart of Tad's adversary. Tad is tried for the killing. We of his family are desolate to learn he is convicted and sentenced to 14 years in prison. Then a dwarf female taxi driver, stunted and ugly, comes on the scene. I refuse her at first. But she persuades me to use her cab. She takes me to where my other son, Pier, lies dying? dead? apparently bludgeoned over the ear with a baseball bat. His brains are seeping out like cream cheese." And "I am in a prison cell. Nothing to do but beat my son to death. I beat my son to death. Then watch as the mosquitoes attack his body until the wardens come in the morning." There were a lot like that.

When Day dreamed about a college boy in a striped bathrobe hanging from a noose, he interpreted the boy as his "writer-self," but noted that the bathrobe resembled mine when I was younger. "And because Tad sees himself as a writer too, I am reinforced in two thoughts, which conflict. To do nothing that will suffocate my nascent self as writer; and nothing that will strangle his ambitions likewise, or his opportunities. The conflict here is that fatherly success might obstruct the son. There are plenty of examples of

that. But note also three male generations of successful artists in the Wyeth clan." A few years later, he dreamed that I
was "scornful" of his "writing and of Asian women in my
life. Sad feeling of my diminishment vis a vis him."

I wasn't scornful of his writing, and I had no idea about
the Asian women. But I did feel that it wasn't easy playing squash against him. Day often griped about his opponent's behavior, stories I didn't question, even though he
was grudging about lets, because he was generally so fair-
minded. Then a tournament opponent of mine asked for a
referee before we'd even started, because he'd once played
Day. And a squash partner of Day's from Buffalo, the play-
wright A. R. Gurney, told me, "He would infuriate me
because he'd try to beat you even when you were warming
up. He'd hit ten shots to himself and then give you one."
Day simply had to win.

In his early fifties, he made it to number 15 in the United
States. Then he wrote a haiku in a Honolulu hotel room:

WHO?
Gimpy dry old man
Lurching into view, hotel
Mirror: oh, myself.

I began doing yoga every morning, dragging my body to the
dog run: upward, downward, junkyard. After six months of
intensive exercise to remediate my intensive exercise, my
tendons relaxed and my cramps diminished.

I spent my lunch hours studying videos of the Egyp-
tian pro Amr Shabana. Shabana, a slight, skittery lefty who
clasped his racquet high on the handle, like a chef carving

a roast, was everything I wanted to be on-court—gracious, graceful, unpredictable, thirty-three. I tried to absorb his catlike movement and deceptive, explosive swing, the way he imposed himself through cumulative pressure, conducting the points.

Richard Chin, the pro at the Harvard Club, kept urging me to pronate my forearm rather than my wrist. Uh-huh. A banty Yoda from Guyana, Richard had a game predicated on getting to every ball, hitting a perfect lob, and regaining the T. Playing him was like contracting dengue fever: for a while, you hurt all over, and then you lost the will to live. He peppered me with technical pointers and found games for me when I traveled, but his chief role was to remind me, in a warm and helpful tone, of all the ways in which I sucked. At the beginning of my quest, I lost in the finals of the Milt Russ Invitational, a tournament Richard hosted for veteran players. The match was close until the fourth game, but Richard just shook his head. "You really think hitting roll corners *from the front of the court* is the way to go?" he said. "I mean, Jesus, Tad! Jesus!"

I began recording my matches on an iPad to identify my other weaknesses. During the playback, I found myself rooting hard for me. I also saw that I was slow returning to the T; that I sometimes took an unaccountable hop before setting off, like Wile E. Coyote band-sawing his legs in mid-air; and that when I hit my backhand crosscourt my shoulder kept on going, yanking me in the wrong direction. The best that could be said was that I sometimes got to balls that looked out of reach, chasing them down with a stompy-footed grunt.

More jarring was the evidence of my mood and character: my default expression was Notre-Dame gargoyle. I didn't curse, much, unless you count "goddammit," but I did occasionally throw my racquet. Usually, this was a gentle toss: committing the ashes of a loved one to the deep. But every six months or so I'd hurl it at the wall—then collect the mutilated frame, feeling like a horse's ass.

Devastatingly, the tapes also revealed what Adam Walker, a Brooklyn pro, had recently warned me about. After we played, he'd said, "You're hitting drops and boasts too early. You're trying to get *out* of the point when squash is all about staying *in* it. Bang, bang, bang, scrape it back, bang, run, hang in there, and the other guy makes a mistake." This was Richard Chin's theme, too: squash is about endurance and sangfroid, about accepting everything your opponent throws at you with the appearance of imperturbability, until he loses heart. But *there*, and *there*, and again *there*, I could see where I'd failed the test.

Deep in the match, when your heart is hammering and your legs begin to seize, fatigue sweeps your mind clean. Your limbic system, freaked out by all the incoming alarms, rashly orders, "Whack it just above the tin! No, no—*above* the tin!" Even the pros make tired errors, but they make them much later in the point. Fatigue exposed my fear of not keeping up, of being the sickly caribou that gets cut from the herd—which provoked the panicky behavior that identified me as the sickly caribou.

I'd thought of myself as someone who hung in. I'd won grueling matches on willpower alone—a determination simply to stay upright, like Toshiro Mifune stuck full of arrows. Yet some stealth riptide had carried me away from my self-image, and I'd become the guy who petered out.

The gap between who I thought I was and the iPad double everyone else saw was the precise measure of my disarray.

I introduced Walker and Addie to squash when they were two, hitting with them most weekends. Addie, a lefty who'd already mastered the monkey bars, capered about, indifferent to the fate of her swooping forehands. A few years later, when she began doing the Robot as she went to serve, Walker watched in bewilderment. For reasons of his own, he'd started wearing a gray-and-yellow wet suit with matching goggles, which made him look like an old-timey Channel swimmer. He liked batting the ball to himself over and over, but he also loved to mix it up unexpectedly, throwing in drop shots from everywhere against all reason, just as I do.

I wanted them to love the game without feeling pressure to be good, or to surpass me, or even to love it just because I did. I wanted it all for them, Sunday after Sunday for years—but they probably learned more from two months of lessons with Cece Cortes, one of my regular partners, who'd just left the tour at number 62 in the world. Cece's swing was classic and correct, her manner encouraging, and her agenda simple: instruction.

As a parent, you can't have a simple agenda. Even as I encouraged Addie to focus—*If you're going to swing, why not hit the ball?*—I also thought, *Wouldn't it be great not to be so attached to outcome?* And Walker's obsessiveness, his hopeful practicing, seemed to me both admirable and heartbreaking. Does anyone ever get all he wants from a game? Amanda snapped a photo of him crouched behind the court, racquet in hand, studying me. His utter susceptibility—

Is this right? Is this how you do it?—filled me with a love close to terror.

Squash with Addie and Walker.

I first wondered if Day was slipping in 2000, when he was in his late sixties. On Labor Day morning, I drove him from Wainscott to Manhattan in his station wagon; after I got out at my place, he'd drive on to Villanova. He had to go to the bathroom, so I gave him the key to my apartment and dropped him out front while I looked for a parking spot. When I walked back a minute later, he was pissing on the corner of my building. At 9:00 A.M. On a busy street. Was he marking his territory, in some bizarre way? Or had he momentarily lost the plot? We didn't discuss it— I wouldn't have known what to say—and he took the car key and drove off.

I thought about that morning again at Christmas in 2011, when Day had to steady himself with both hands to sit, used "adjure" for "abjure," and began eating before everyone was at the table. "Do you want to wait for us?" Timmie asked. He looked up, startled, spare rib at his lips.

In the fall of 2015, when he was eighty-four, he fell while walking a trail near his house. At Christmas, he fell again. In early January, Dominic Hughes, the pro at his squash club, noticed that Day was dressing himself with paralyzing slowness and drove him to Bryn Mawr Hospital. The tests revealed only what we already knew: pre-diabetes and pancytopenia, or low blood-cell levels, along with chronic kidney disease, acute gout, and intracranial arachnoid cysts—nothing noxious enough to be knocking him down. His diagnosis was a shruggy catchall: "Generalized weakness." But the resident took me aside: "Your father is experiencing physically what we often see mentally in patients with Alzheimer's. The decline has been happening for a while, but he's hidden it by the equivalent of writing notes to himself and simplifying his questions and answers. A few days ago, he could no longer maintain the masquerade."

I began playing squash four times a week, pushing my limits, and "ghosting" after light matches—making two- or three-step glides into the corners of the court, then springing back to the T, over and over and over, to improve my speed, fitness, and efficiency of movement. The goal was to be so catlike I couldn't hear my footfalls, but I sounded like Captain Ahab stumping to the fo'c'sle.

I also scheduled matches with better players. One was Will Carlin, who was my age and even more of a tinkerer and a self-improver. In his twenties, he'd been America's best player, fifty-third in the world. Stocky, intense, a stickler, he was armor-plated in fitness—his resting pulse rate, at one point, was a whalelike twenty-eight. He liked to drill after we played. I'd never been big on drills, but with Will I preferred them to our matches, because the way his warmth and thoughtfulness contracted in competition reminded me uncomfortably of myself. So we'd trade baby drops and crosscourt volleys. I'd have an occasional glint of brilliance—a moment when I lunged just right, held my shot to freeze him, then feathered in a drop to the nick, the delicious spot where the floor and the side wall join and the ball rolls out dead. But Will's game was sounder in almost every aspect.

I wasn't trying to be world class, just to improve to the point where I could play the game well without even thinking about it. I was trying to achieve immersion. But it's tricky, trying to foster a feeling that's predicated on a lack of self-awareness. You realize the joy of immersion only later, because at the time you're too immersed.

For instance: a summer afternoon at my grandparents' farm in Woodstock, when I am six. After a hike to a dell of fern and hemlock, Grandma Tim leads us across a stone wall into a grove of sugar maples, where a spring had been channeled into a brimming iron hoop. When I lean over it, the clouds in the water's dark surface become my face, as in a destiny mirror of legend. The water is intoxicatingly cold, and the enameled-tin cup clangs on the cistern like a gong.

And: walking down a garbagey Boston street on a spring morning, rain pending, as someone above throws up a sash. I am twenty, and I have just landed an extremely uncompetitive internship at *Partisan Review*, the first rung on a ladder that will lead, I suddenly believe, to a career as a writer. I am wearing my favorite navy-blue sweater with white bird's-eye checks, unaware that it will later become every costume designer's idea of early-eighties crap fashion.

And: sitting in a window bay of the Empire State Building, at night, with Natalie. I am twenty-five, and oblivious to all the ways she is wrong for me, oblivious to her sorrows, her waywardness, her alcoholism. A group of us have smuggled Scotch and a stereo into a friend's office on the seventy-seventh floor, and "Wishing Well" is booming, that giddy drum-machine-and-bass hook. I wear contact lenses then, and one is killing me, so I take it out and cradle it in my palm as we kiss, enveloped by her geranium scent. With my nearsighted eye I see her soft mouth and glacier-blue eye made enormous, while my corrected eye sees the Chrysler Building and the blazing city beyond: close-up zooming to master shot, the way New York can suddenly open itself to you for a moment, when you're young.

And: running barefoot on a beach in Australia, near Wollongong, at twenty-six. I am traveling the world for a year, running everywhere to keep fit and explore. A low horizon, a gray sea, a hard flat wide beach, and the soft rain promised in Boston six years earlier falling now. I run for miles, skimming over the packed sand. The world is a treadmill and I can run forever.

Me on a hay wagon in Woodstock.

After his hospital stay, Day noted in a letter to Timmie, "I see my handwriting is small today: a factor of hospital psychology and patient humility." Yet he insisted that all was well. Then, walking out to pick up the mail, he fell head-first onto his driveway. Bleeding copiously, having somehow locked himself out of the house, he staggered to a neighbor's. It took nine stitches to close his forehead, and the doctors gave him a cane.

We drove down that Friday night. Traditionally, Day would be in his study among his books, but after Mom died, he'd succumbed to the acronymous pleasures of *CSI* and *SVU* and *NCIS*. I joined him on the couch for *Law & Order*. The plastic lenses in his eyes, from his cataract surgeries, shone in the TV's glow.

After watching Sam Waterston speechify about corruption, I asked, "What appeals to you about this show?"

"I like law and I like order," Day said, his eyes on a mattress commercial. "Order, more. And TV at night was a habit I got into at fifty-five." I was going to quibble—more like day and night, and seventy-five—but he went on, "And now *you're* reaching that age. The age of inflexibility, when no new habits form."

"Maybe having children when you're older keeps that at bay for a while, because you have to enter a child's frame of mind," I suggested. "They see the world through a telescope that makes small things huge, and Amanda and I get to borrow it."

"Maybe," he said, doubtfully. "We'll see."

In between touring all the Philadelphia sights I'd hated as a kid—Betsy Ross's house, the Liberty Bell—we bought Walker four pairs of pants at Uniqlo. Back at Day's, Walker announced a fashion show. When he made an entrance in his new chinos, I was on my phone, checking Twitter. When I finally looked up and saw his expression, I felt so ashamed I couldn't breathe.

At bedtime, Addison informed me, "You have a bald patch."

"It's a bald *spot*," I said. " 'Patch' is for a color, like gray."

"You have that, too."

If we avoid the aged, we'll never die—an instinct that the cultural anthropologist Ernest Becker termed "terror management." He wrote, "The irony of man's condition is that the deepest need is to be free of the anxiety of death and annihilation; but it is life itself which awakens it, and so we must shrink from being fully alive." Your job as a parent is to uproot that anxiety, or at least to prune it back. Your job is to lie like a condemned man.

Addison and Walker didn't seem to notice that anything had changed with Day, and he didn't seem to notice them at all. Later, though, I'd learn that he wrote, "My dear guests are gone, but their vivid memories linger. Walker and Addie each slipped between my knees to give me long hugs, and promised they would miss me. I miss them."

Back home, when I explained the word "timeless" to the kids over breakfast, as I was improvising another chapter in the saga of Sergio, the Extremely Sharp-Eyed Mole, Addison asked, "Are we timeless?"

"Absolutely!" I lied.

She leaned in a few months later, after we laughed at the same thing—a businessman tripping over his own briefcase—and told me, "The only bad thing about growing up is that we get closer and closer and closer to you passing away." I laughed again, wincing. She added, reassuringly, "But we'll keep pictures of you."

At fifty-two, I conceived a grand unified theory of squash. I was warming the ball up with a Swede named Anders Wahlstedt, an amiable art dealer who was once number 18 in the world. In truth, Anders, in his fluorescent-orange shirt and iridescent-green socks, was doing most of the ball warming. He cracked forehands from a sturdy crouch, his swing full and flowing, the ball cannoning down the side wall to expire in the back corner, repetitious as a GIF. These perfect rails, which are hard even to return, let alone do much with, are known as "dying lengths." Anders calls his high-ordnance game his "bombardment." The word I prefer hearing, in his flat tones, is "Motherfocker." Very occasionally, when his tactics aren't working, he lets out a

"Motherfocker!" and shakes his fists at the ceiling, like Job in a silent movie.

I was thinking, *How is it that I can stay on the court with Anders?* Though he pulverized me when he was moving well, our matches were usually close, and I eked out a victory now and then. That's when I conceived the Hourglass Analogy. At Anders's peak, in 1988—when he and I were in the top bulb of the hourglass—he'd have blown me off the court. In our seventies, his fundamentals will again make him invincible.

But now, in our fifties, we're sliding down the neck of the hourglass together. And during this interlude I can still get to a lot of his shots, surviving long enough to counterattack. So Anders repeatedly buries me deep, making me run faster and lunge harder and twist more rapidly than anyone else. And when he wins a long point late in the match he bounds to the service box to get on with it, while I'm rubbing my sweaty palm in meditative circles on the wall, trying not to resemble a sheepdog in a hot car.

Anders denies me time to sharpshoot by extending and exhausting me. I deny him time to calibrate his bombardment by slipping in volley drops or a wrong-footing boast. It's all about denying time.

Amanda endured my obsession the way you endure a car alarm, expecting it to stop any minute. "How are the hammies?" she'd ask, gravely; it's possible that I'd occasionally discussed the state of my hamstrings in excessive detail. Now, deciding that the only way out was through, she gave me a Christmas present of a lesson with Peter Nicol. Peter, a lithe Scottish lefty, was the world's top player for much of the late nineties and early aughts, a tireless retriever with a remarkable ability to analyze his opponent's game. After batting the ball to me for thirty seconds, he knew all my weaknesses. He demonstrated how cramped my swing was—it resembled a feeble defense against a gang of pickpockets—then had me stand farther from the ball and throw the bottom edge of my racquet at it, for more control and also, curiously, more power.

There was a coherent worldview at work, one entailing less work for me and more for my opponent. The farther I stayed from the ball, the closer I stayed to the T, and the more correctly I hit the ball, the faster I sprang back from it. After an hour of hitting, I suddenly began to crack my backhand rails down the wall and recoil smoothly. It felt like a molecular shift, an upgrade in how my body fit into the world. I was recording the lesson on my iPad, and when I played it back, I looked almost—what's the word? . . . *fluid.* Then we played a game, and I won, 11–6. You could argue that Peter let me win, but only if you wanted to be a total jerk.

Afterward, he said, "You're very coachable. If you work on the form, you can get your basics up to the level of your drop shots, and then you'll be very tough indeed." His patently overgenerous compliments filled me with joy. I practiced a more capacious swing in the elevator, on the subway, even in the shower: striding in, throwing the bottom edge, bouncing back. I hit some superb shower backhands, burying the ball by Addison's red tugboat.

Six months into my regimen, I entered my first U.S. Nationals. Day was seventy-five and had played in numerous

Nationals when he finally earned his championship ball. As he told the story, a hard serve gained him a weak return, and all the time in the world to put it away, but he slammed it into the tin. He played that sitter over and over in his head—"I either drop it deftly or smash it carefully"—but even in his do-overs, he couldn't quite decide how to finish it. In his journals, he acknowledged that he'd actually squandered *six* championship points: "To me it remains a scalding fact."

The tournament courts, in Stamford, Connecticut, were bisected by a long corridor. The show courts, featuring the twentysomethings in the Open division, America's best, were at one end, and the elders at the other. As I walked toward the outer courts, players time-lapsed before me, graying and thickening, growing encumbered with face shields, elbow sleeves, and knee braces, then freezing altogether at the T. Mobility is the game's cruel prerequisite: of the fourteen guys in the seventies draw, only two could really run.

Day should have been on the last court, with the eighty-year-olds, but he wasn't. For several years, he'd played with a group called the Older Guys, of whom he was the Oldest. When he began falling, the Older Guys grew concerned, and finally Dominic, the pro, called me. He called me, rather than Day, for the same reason I stalled for an hour before I called Day. It's terrible to have to say, "You've hit your last ball."

I explained, as gently as I could, that "Dominic, regretfully, was conveying the sentiments of the group. They believe it's time."

"Well, I don't believe that it's time! And I am not

going to be bullied into retirement according to Dominic Hughes's schedule!"

"I understand," I said. "And I wish it all weren't so. But Dominic isn't really the referee here."

"I know, Taddio," he said, sadly. "And I accede." His instant capitulation was more dismaying than his fury.

I won my first match, lost my second, won two matches in the consolations, and then lost to a classy player from Massachusetts. These mixed results briefly boosted me to number 10 in the country. I made a note to be thrilled, but, after five matches in less than forty-eight hours, I felt like a fossil hastily reassembled from a tar pit. Will Carlin, who'd lost in the semis, came over in the locker room to commiserate. "We're pretty good players in our neighborhood," he said. "But there are a lot of neighborhoods out there."

If you love a demanding task, one that requires both discipline and talent—shooting hoops, playing drums, writing code—you eventually discover an innate boundary: you can apprehend real virtuosity, especially as it's used to best you, but you can't quite incorporate it. You will never be more than almost great. The same wistfulness I now felt also crossed Will's face when he recalled winning a single point against the immortal Jahangir Khan, Mohibullah Khan's cousin, and Richard Chin's face when he recounted his brief match with the standout Ramy Ashour. Yet the truly great players sacrifice so much that they stare back at us with equal longing. Or so we console ourselves.

The locker room, full of swaddled bodies dusted with baby powder, is a kind of late-life nursery. When I played in one Milt Russ tournament, Walker cocked an ear to all the talk of middle-aged twinges, then summarized it as "Hey, Bobby, how's your body? Can you still pee out of it?"

As I was changing to play a few years ago, the chatter, so often about hips and backs and knees, was about the virtues of dying on-court. Dinny, in his seventies, mentioned a great of yesteryear, Pete Bostwick, whose father had a heart attack while playing polo at seventy-two.

Ted, a player my age, shook his head: "You die at that age and no one remembers you, no one comes to your funeral."

Another elder, knotting his wingtips, murmured, "You won't feel that way when you're seventy."

Dinny asked, "So when do you want to go, and how?" I gathered my racquets, heading out.

"I don't know," Ted said, "but I want it to be quick and painless and soon."

"What about lightning?" I heard Dinny ask, in the distance. "Have you thought about lightning?"

In the summer of 2016, I noticed a slow burn in my belly. After two weeks, I went to my GP. He prodded my abdomen with two fingers, frowned, and said, "I think you have appendicitis. Some people have a shy appendix that hides behind the intestine, and they develop a slow leak." An MRI confirmed his diagnosis, and I was in the emergency room two hours later.

The MRI also revealed that I'd been born without a left kidney. My wisdom teeth had never come in, I'd had my tonsils out, and a leaky aortic valve made my heart murmur with every beat—how many serviceable organs remained? Feeling ransacked, I grumbled to the surgeon, a flinty Russian, about the broth-only diet he'd put me on. He snorted and said, "Nobody ever died of starvation in America."

When I got home, appendix gone, I realized that while I was in the hospital, I'd also lost my iPad.

I went down in the semis of the following year's Milt Russ in five. The match left me with a grapefruit-sized cyst behind my left knee that took three months of physical therapy to fix, and with a locker-room conversation starter: my newfangled knee brace. When I was younger, taking a break like that made my body feel less banged up. Now it felt awful, like detoxing.

The year after, I advanced to the final—against Will Carlin. An overflow crowd of eight gathered, including Amanda, Walker, and Addison. Will, wearing an all-black outfit and a knee brace of his own, looked stern and focused, but I'd finally beaten him the previous week in practice. I edged him in the first, 13–11.

Lobbing my backhand intelligently, monotonously, Will took the next game at 7 and the third at 9. During the break, Addison whispered, "Dad, can you play better? Do something hard and fast and then sneaky!" I laughed and played better, but suddenly Will had two match balls at 10–8. I decoyed him in for a backhand drop and flicked it crosscourt. At 9–10, I thumped a series of forehand rails and then whipped a crosscourt by him. Another crosscourt got me a game ball, and a backhand volley—a nick at the perfect time—closed it out.

Before long I was down, 7–5, in the fifth. Walker was anxiously unwinding the grip on his racquet. I hit two tins, then, after a wipe-and-stroll to regain my breath, two quick winners. Will went up 10–8, but I made it 9–10. He punished my hard serve and maintained the advantage as we traded rails. At last, he pulled me wide with a crosscourt, then cut in a volley kill that I lunged to scrape back— a fraction late. As Will threw up his arms, I felt a terrible pang. We embraced and staggered off the court, and the pang diminished. I'd stayed in there—more than stayed in there—and still lost. But by God it was fun.

Addison turned to dance and cross-country, hurt her foot, then took up singing. Walker migrated to soccer, spending hours shooting on an empty net. Neither, it seems, is going to love squash as I do.

That love has only grown, to my surprise. I haven't hurled a racquet in years. And I played well at a recent Nationals, coming in sixth, which I think of as the bottom of the top, though it's really the top of the middle. After I lost my last match, Richard Chin gave me one of his pep talks: "You wouldn't have won even if you were playing well, but you were terrible. I mean, just terrible." Anders Wahlstedt lost in the final, despite being up two games against Dominic Hughes, whom he'd have trounced when they were young. Afterward Anders stood in the center of the locker room, naked and stricken. Finally, he sighed and started for the showers—then paused to ask, "What happened out there, Tad?"

The game never quite lets you seize it whole. Some days, I hit nothing but Peter Nicol backhands, and others I tattoo the tin. So I came into the Milt Russ in November with no expectations. I won my first three matches and felt reasonably quick and strong, but Will was again waiting in the final. He'd scorched through his draw, and when we started I could see why. He'd been working with a pro on his move-

ment, and he was a half step quicker and a hair more confident. He closed me out fast, without nearly enough drama.

I've always admired Samuel Beckett's maxim "Ever
tried. Ever failed. No matter. Try again. Fail again. Fail better." But I had failed worse. Richard Chin said—well, you
can guess. It occurred to me, during a long, long shower,
that I might have passed my peak. Maybe the previous
year's match against Will was the best I'd ever play, and I
was now on the far slope of the mountain.

I'd remember that feeling when I found Day's last set
of training notebooks, which extended to 2015. I paged
through them, watching his sit-ups decline to sixteen and
his push-ups fall to four. At seventy-seven, he ran 200
meters in 58 seconds. And then, before he could no longer
break a minute, he stopped running.

Oversight

IN THE spring of 2019, we FaceTimed with Day. In the seven months since Timmie and I had interviewed him, he'd faded from cane to walker. When we pinged Mary, they were playing gin rummy. No longer his girlfriend, as she hadn't wanted to become his nurse, she was still a frequent visitor. "He can't resist picking up an ace, even if it doesn't help him," she reported, handing Day the phone. His owlish pupils filled the screen, much too close; he'd never grasped how to see himself on FaceTime. We'd used Mary as a go-between because Day no longer emailed, hadn't got the hang of his cellphone, and, on his landline, now gave mostly terse and equivocal responses: "Fair to good," "Not bad," "More or less."

His voicemails once had the opposite issue. Three or four minutes long, they'd encompass the weather—"It's a bracing fall day, with an early snowfall predicted for tomorrow, Monday, enough to bring the plows around, certainly, and enough to remind me to bring in more wood from the woodpile, in that handsome dark brown carry bag that Mom got me some years ago"——encounters at the post office, and meetings he'd had at the Foreign Policy Research Institute. "So, again, it's Dorie/Day, here in the former Pennsylvania Colony, founded by William Penn in 1681, calling on Veterans Day to wish you peace from domestic strife as well as the avoidance of foreign entanglement."

Our faces helped focus him. But we were getting only nostril, so Mary leaned in: "Dorie, you need to——"

"Don't pick at me!"

"You know best!"

As Walker and Addison chattered away, Day eyed them as if they were clown fish in an aquarium. He got distracted by a bird outside his window—a cardinal?—and soon they were talking to his right shoulder. Then to empty sky.

The day I got my driver's license, at sixteen, I volunteered to take our station wagon to the Springfield Mall, less than a mile away, to pick up a ring that Mom had had resized. When I strode up to the jewelry store's counter, the salesman drooped his phone's receiver in my direction: "It's your *mother*."

"Oh, darling," she said. "I just wanted to make sure you made it safely!"

I longed to live an unmonitored life. Mom was all over me, and Day kept watch, too, though he was loath to confront me too directly. In my senior year of high school, I snuck a corkscrew and a bottle of Riesling from our pantry into the station wagon and drove to a party. A week later, he observed, musingly, "Someone left a corkscrew in the glove box."

"Um, yeah, me," I said. I thought he might engage—jaw a bit about drinking and driving, show some concern—but he just knit his brow. "Oversight" is a Janus word, like "buckle" or "cleave"; it means both supervision and neglect.

My class chose Day as our commencement speaker, and I felt stricken. *In a public forum, he could address me privately.* He began by mentioning that he'd just bought an Emmylou Harris record, a name-check that elicited crickets. He went on, nonetheless, to chide us for quoting so many singers and bands on our yearbook pages (I'd quoted Paul Simon). The Grateful Dead's "What a long, strange trip it's been" had certainly been overworked; a few keggers do not a Summer of Love make. But Day's observation that in college "popular songs, I suspect, should subside in their significance, as lullabies, once important in your lives, have dwindled in memory" was kind of snotty.

His preferred mode of communication was mail: a letter not only foreclosed an immediate rejoinder but could be revised until it was nearly rejoinder proof. When I was four, Mom noted that when I saw one of his heavily edited drafts, I said, "What's wrong with that letter? It looks like it was in a fight." In the spring of my sophomore year in college, one of Day's letters concluded, "I write here in capital letters the words SUMMER JOB, not to goad your conscience, which I know is always alert, but as a little tick to help along whatever planning mechanism you have going." The following spring, he quoted Shaw—"Hell is to drift, heaven to steer"—as he urged me to frame my summer and fall plans and detail them in a letter to him "laying out a three- to five-year plan."

I sensed his disappointment that I had no plan to be a historian or a spiritual pilgrim. Day's sensibility was essentially pagan, but religion's dignifying narrative reassured him that life was more than an instinctive misery or—worse—a joke. He and Mom dragged us to church most Sundays, but he never tried to proselytize us, so I'm not sure how deeply his heart was in it. I liked the hymns and the sturdy oak pews and the candlelight service on Christmas Eve, but I hated being bundled into a coat and tie and admonished from the pulpit. When I was in college, a devout friend was dismayed to discover that I didn't believe my life had any ordained purpose: "You're just a happy nihilist!" No. I wasn't happy, for one thing. And I was still seeking the sacred, just not in the neighborhood of God.

Day's deeper concern was that I had no plan at all. After my junior year, when I took a semester off to work at Houghton Mifflin, the publisher, he wrote to say that my decision needed to be "sharply justified philosophically and psychologically to yourself and to us." I just wanted to slow down and grow up a bit, but I think he was afraid that I was taking after Grandpa Ted. Recently, when Day and I had found ourselves watching the World Series of Poker on TV, he'd narrowed his eyes at the million-dollar wagers and observed that he'd never played poker after the night, freshman year, when he lost $130: "Because my father was twice kicked out of Yale for gambling, I was on guard against that weakness in myself."

A few years after college, I drove across the United States for six weeks with my friend Rich. When we hit a place like Barstow, California, we'd head to the Tower Records to ask the guy behind the counter where he hung out, which led us to a lot of dive bars and skeevy museums. It was a pretty good way to discover Americana. But when I told Day about our m.o., he said, "It does not sound as if your trip is densely textured."

In 1989, he wrote me in Jakarta, "Now that you are at last in Asia, is your definition of culture the same as before? (I am not implying that you have wrestled or should grapple with that problem in an Eliotic manner. But I am suggesting that your sense of the potentialities of souls and whole societies may somehow shift, subtly or massively, in ways that are distinctively your own.)"

Indonesia had changed Day, and he wanted it to change me, too. Years later, in his magnum opus, *Indonesian Destinies*, in which he interwove the country's political history with his own experiences there, he recalled driving through Jakarta on the back of an Irish friend's motorcycle, "through urban stench, smoke, spice, rot, and shit," weaving "in and out among men pedaling *becaks*, diesel buses farting black particulates, wounded private automobiles, limping taxis, occasional carriages with knobby-kneed horses, and humans of all ages with shoulder yokes or long carry-poles, bearing live things, or once live things." And he wrote about the rice terraces of Sulawesi, "Sesean, for me, is the most beautiful mountain valley in the world—steep and green in far more dramatic ways than Bali or Italy. I descended ledges of padi in knife-edge awareness that I might never again know such dizzy natural happiness."

In my late twenties and early thirties, I reported from overseas for *Harper's, Esquire,* and *Outside*. Among those stories were one filed from Indonesia and two from the Philippines. But I was determined to understand those countries in my own way. I might arrive at the same conclusions Day had, but I would do independent research. I would show my work.

Rare photo of Day and me alone together, Oslo, 1979.

Whenever Day had a moment, on a boat or a train or in a remote hotel, he'd begin a letter to us in his flowing hand. He had a noticing eye for flora; was exacting about diacritical marks; and loved to flash out arresting facts about his locale and its history, such as that Bismarck was the father of social security. A talk he'd given was often enclosed: "Changing American Values, Since 1965"; "Morality and American Foreign Policy"; "American Religiosity and Civil Religion." While his benchmark was America, his points of comparison were ubiquitous: "The population of Iceland is 250,000, about the same as Toledo, Ohio"; "Ireland is the only cold tropical country"; "There are 23,000 native Caymanians. They speak a rich broad Caribbean English, unhurried and unemphatic, except for a Gaelic lilt at the ends of sentences."

Like a Toynbee or a Harari, he inclined to epic sweep. He photocopied his interminate letters and mailed or faxed them to all of us, until Timmie said she would no longer read anything on which she was cc'd. His twelve-, fifteen-, twenty-page analyses of cultures we were unlikely to experience and people we'd almost certainly never meet seemed aimed at the larger audience of posterity. Though he often lodged a personal p.s. sideways in the margin, to close the distance between us, his letters began to have the opposite effect. In 1994, he wrote from Beijing, "Assisted by an extraordinary interpreter I had a conversation as guest of honor with seven Chinese of the (new think-tank) Council on Policy and Strategy in Shanghai. With Golden Dynasty wine and a long business meeting behind us, the conversational and speculative stakes rose until I was able to ask the senior economist present (who as a boy genius physicist had had a paper submitted to Einstein, but then joined the anti-Japanese and anti-KMT forces, and for the sake of his country became an economist (two Ph.D's))—'Is there a single unit of energy that may be defined as operative in both material forces and in social dynamics?' This question was aimed to suggest that Marx had failed in his effort to establish a philosophic 'metabolism with nature.' It succeeded instead, however, in our arriving at agreement on a formula to define the most promising society: $d/c + e$ (where d = energy spent on individuals developing themselves and their institutions, c = what they ingest and consume, and e = what they display and exhibit)." *Is this going to be on the test?*

When I started keeping a journal, I also started gathering my mail into orange Amberg letter boxes, alphabetically by date. Day, whose Amberg armada filled several shelves, had given me my first box. His letters went into it, but I began to tune out his correspondence.

In college, I played backgammon and bridge for low stakes and was a Republican for a week. In my early twenties, I tried on bonsai trees, billowing shirts from Brooks Brothers, and a John Cusack vibe. Then, living in TriBeCa with my college roommates from France and Argentina, I became a Eurotrash wannabe. Gamine women were always confiding to me how mad they were for George or Pablo, and I hoped that sympathetic listening might reroute some of the ambient adoration. There were dinners at Odeon; drinks on roofs, the fire door propped with a cinder block; lofts hazy with Gauloises. But it never quite took. I couldn't drape a scarf in a negligent circle, like a fallen halo.

In 1987, I was an editor at *Spy,* a satirical magazine that had taken off. I invited Mom and Day to come to New York for our first anniversary party, a black-tie affair, so they could see me in my element. Day came, solo, and mixed easily with my friends. A week later, I was dancing at El Morocco with George's girlfriend and she said, "You dance just like your father!" Seeing my scowl, she hastily added, "But better!"

When Day was traveling in Turkey for EEF, building a network there, I put him in touch with a friend, a well-connected Anglophile Turk who wrote for *Spy.* They got on well, but afterward Day invoked Turgenev: "The cosmopolitan is a nonentity." I urged him to read "American

Express," a James Salter story about American cosmopolitans that I thought magic. Salter's Frank said "Women fall in love when they get to know you. Men are just the opposite. When they finally know you they're ready to leave." Day wasn't interested in that. He observed that Frank was decadent (true) and that Salter was frigid (false). Salter, who wrote elsewhere, "Life is contemptuous of knowledge; it forces it to sit in the anterooms, to wait outside. Passion, energy, lies: these are what life admires."

"You can't build a society on Salter," he said.

"Is that the goal of art?"

"It ought to be."

Unawares, I had begun to audition father figures. Graydon Carter, one of *Spy*'s founding editors, was enormously charming. He wore red suspenders and roamed the office with a sort of dashing waddle. Hilarious himself, he listened to you expectantly, egging you on so he could throw his head back and laugh. We edited heavily at *Spy*, honing every dart, and Graydon would remind me, "Most of the people we write about *deserve* to be cut down to size." Yet he wasn't a scold or a killjoy. While he gave plenty of advice—"Never pin your self-worth on being the youngest at anything. Because you grow older."—he didn't need me to emulate him, or to live the life he wished he'd led. I savored the hearty way he called me "Tadorific" and his Wodehousian hangover cure (it involved a raw egg whipped in Worcestershire sauce, and it didn't work), as well as his instinct to attack humbug, and his contrition when he went too far, as he often did. Most of all, I savored his belief that I had a distinctive voice.

In 1992, Graydon became the editor of *Vanity Fair*. He

twice offered me a job, as an editor and later as a writer, but I was leery of the corner booth and the society murder, that Weimar frolic. As his tenure extended to twenty-five years and his bespoke suits and silver hair fulfilled the augury of those suspenders, I came to suspect that he'd needled the rich and famous at *Spy* less to deflate them than to inflate himself. What I'd instinctively rejected, then, was the warping potential of my yearning for prominence. I longed to be known, but only if my work rose of its own merits. Maybe Graydon knew all that and was amused by my naïveté. When I ran into him at Condé Nast he'd cry "Tadorific!" and smile, across the crowded elevator, as if we shared a secret.

In the early nineties, Day underwent a second round of Jungian therapy, with a female analyst this time. It reinforced his habit of discerning controlling motifs in art and life—the Harry Potter films' obsession with wands, for instance. "In the end," he wrote in his journals, "Harry's younger, purer symbolic phallus gives off more energy than Voldemort's aged and overcompromised symbolic phallus."

He considered becoming a psychotherapist, but was discouraged by the extensive training required. So he practiced on the psyche he knew best. He wrote his analyst to say, "I see my own 'self' as having three distinct, non-orthogonal, but (at my best) highly coordinate functions." There was the inner self, the religious self, and the family self, "as evident in my novel; in my work at Swarthmore, putting back together several constituencies alienated in multiple ways; in my work at EEF with a global 'family' of fellows. I seek to evoke harmony and productivity among external elements." Somehow his family self still didn't encompass his actual family.

I'd always been leery of therapy, because I needed it so. For years, I could work out that I was depressed only by my response when friends made that diagnosis. It was like waking to amnesia in a hospital, studying your bleeding fists, then noticing that the doctors have taken shelter behind cops with riot shields. *Whoever I am, I must not like being examined.* My childhood wish for solitude had been granted, and it stunk. Grudgingly, hoping to pick up a few tips in a few months and be on my way, I finally started seeing a Freudian analyst.

Sylvia helped me realize how my need for attention had figured into my career; writing enabled me to mount a performative version of myself. I could overlay *The New Yorker*'s ennobling font, TNY Adobe Caslon Pro Regular, on my interior Comic Sans. Yet publication brought me little joy. It only increased my habitual apprehension. If someone challenged my work I'd feel dismal—but it was even worse if no one responded at all. Exiled onto the sunporch every time a piece came out, I'd try to escape it again by writing the next one.

When Mom got sick, in 1995, I'd been in therapy for two years, and it felt like time to put it to use. I took Day to lunch and brought up our relationship, and my wish for it to be better, freer, more heartfelt. His cheeks blazed as he asked questions, but he didn't volunteer much. Two days later, his letter arrived:

> I was happy to talk with you about family and feeling; and angles of time felt and seen differently; and

anger, how to use it as a resource, and how to "govern" it, to use your excellent word. I hope the conversation was as useful to you as it was illuminating to me. I do not imagine you found much wisdom (unlike those coffee-house conversationalists who enjoyed "dipping in the honeypot of Oliver Goldsmith's mind"). Or that you uncovered illuminating secrets (as did the FBI, rummaging in Aldrich Ames' trash bin to discover his true mentality). But I am ready for any such exercise any time that may serve your need, and the joy of familial discourse.

You could read it as encouragement, but I knew that Teflon erudition. I think it was then that I began to give up on Day. I would go my own way, become exquisitely sensitive and self-aware, and surpass him.

But working on myself didn't prove any easier. My New Year's resolutions for 1996, recorded in my journal, were

- Have a book underway by year's end
- Move to a larger apartment
- Stop falling for Salinger heroines—bright, superior, kinder to cats than people

My resolutions for 1997 were virtually identical. 1998, too. I was a walking January gym membership.

When the 2000 Republican convention was held in Philadelphia, Day asked me to come see George W. Bush accept the nomination. I think he thought I might learn something, or perhaps it was just that as a Republican donor he had two tickets and Mom, a lifelong Democrat, had zero interest in attending. In the boozy skyboxes of the First Union Center, home to the Philadelphia Flyers, he introduced me to his circle of moderate Republicans, convivial men with firm handshakes and oyster breath. When Bush decried "the soft bigotry of low expectations," they roared with enthusiasm. I sat silent, doubting.

Day came to detest Bush and his era. Timmie and I coined another bit of shorthand, "I am *not* going to write Donald Rumsfeld's biography!" for Day's jeremiads about American foreign policy. Rumsfeld had chaired EEF from 1986 to 1992, and Day liked him, except on the squash court: "He was a poor loser." When Rumsfeld became Bush's secretary of defense, Day felt duty bound to warn him about some crucial unknown unknowns. Twelve days after 9/11, Day wrote him, "I must say what is clear to me even if it is already obvious to you. Afghanistan has exhausted and defeated every army that entered it. The Afghans themselves have already made rubble of Kabul. The networks like Al Qaeda, in all their national habitats, will not be checked by mega-bombing." In a later note, he warned that "decapitation of leadership in Iraq under the rubric of regional peace-keeping recalls the Anglo-French attempt in 1956 to topple Nasser of Egypt. Result: lonely failure and general hostility." Rumsfeld never replied.

When Day gave the keynote at a policy symposium at Columbia University, in 2005, he said, "We all hoped somehow to have an impact"—in Vietnam—"and of course we did not. Whatever we knew was immaterial to those in power. That feeling of helplessness against bureaucratic deafness is repeated today in Iraq." He later reviewed two Rumsfeld books in *Orbis*, one of them his old friend's memoirs, and described the former secretary as "both 'visceral' and 'provincial.'" So, no, he was not going to write Donald Rumsfeld's biography.

In 2008, he registered as a Democrat and voted for Barack Obama.

In the aughts, I started group therapy with some of Sylvia's other patients. Having grown more comfortable in my skin, I wanted to stop making other people uneasy in theirs—to stop seeming prickly and aloof. The Group's therapist was Paul Klein, a wiry, charismatic man in his fifties. He knew exactly how Leo would feel about what Mark just said to Jenny; he had a panoptic sensitivity. And he liked showing it off. As a father figure, he was part magus, part Vegas. In an early one-on-one, Paul called my attention to Jenny's having remarked that I reminded her of her father. "Tom, with his instinct for the alpha male, saw what was going on," he said, grinning as if we were in cahoots. "Jenny was lifting her rump to you."

I relished Paul's candor and his bonobian cast of mind— the way he made insight seem sexy. He encouraged me to become a therapist, like him; if I made a small shift from a reporter's neutral scrutiny to a shrink's empathetic intervention, I could shape lives. He was tapping my pride in my grasp of emotional dynamics and playing to one of my biggest flaws: my need to appear omniscient.

I began to herd the Group as Paul's unofficial apprentice: Joy, tell your husband you're lonely. Leo, stop presenting yourself as a needy fat kid. Mark, you can't masturbate your way into a relationship. Paul would nod, overpaint the canvas a touch, then add his signature.

A year into it, I went to Los Angeles for a story. Paul videotaped our sessions, so when I got back, I watched the two I'd missed. At our next meeting, I observed that everyone seemed to have had a lot more fun without me. They eagerly explained that that was because I was "dismissive," "a schoolteacher," "an alien doctor" who made them feel "like a butterfly nailed to a wall."

Paul asked how everyone thought this bombardment had affected me. I had always seemed implacable, so the question took them aback. "Hurt?" Joy guessed. "Are you hurt?" My eyes were brimming. "So that's a yes?" I nodded. The last forty minutes was all Kleenex. I had finally joined the Group.

In 2016, after Day began falling, we divvied up his care. Timmie, steeped in medical protocol from her liver transplant, handled the doctors and nurses and dealt with Day's spectacularly negligent housekeeper. Pier hired a bookkeeper, weaned Day off his credit cards, and kept an eye on his accounts. I oversaw the house and his daily upkeep, in consultation with a care manager we'd hired, Janice Duffin. Day, resenting this supervision, called her "O'Duffin," as if she were an Irish cop with a night stick.

That spring, Pier and Timmie and I sat Day down in Mom's garden, where the crocuses had popped up around the stone bull she'd hoped her grandchildren would ride. We told him he wasn't ready to resume driving. When I'd taken him out on some errands, earlier, he'd yelled "Slow down!" or "Turn here!" fifty yards too soon.

"I don't drive at night," he said, testily. "I know my limits."

"We're glad of that," I said, glancing at the others, because Day often drove at night. "We think it's a daytime problem, too, though. And you're not just putting yourself at risk—you could hit a bus full of nuns." He grimaced at this Mom tactic, the hyperbole. Before he could chop his hand sideways to dispatch the notional nuns, I went on. "Why don't you take the adult driving test? Then you'd be certified."

"If I pass the test," he roared, "will you all admit that you were wrong?"

There was a silence. Eventually, I said, "That would lay our concerns to rest."

Pier said, "We don't want you to lose your independence. But in the meantime, Uber is easy to use."

"We'll table the matter till I take the test, then," Day said. He seemed a little sheepish about his outburst. "I appreciate your concern for my well-being."

"And you won't drive until you take it?" I said.

That dogged expression. "Only if I have to."

Day kept driving. When I reproached him, six weeks later, he said he'd never agreed to stop. "How about I don't drive at night?" he offered.

"In our last conversation you said you'd already quit driving at night." He looked surprised—then grinned at his unremembered wiliness. "You have to *promise* to stop driving until the test."

"Very well," he said. "I promise."

"How will I know, when I'm in Brooklyn, that you're not driving?"

"You're going to have to trust me," he said warmly. "The way I've always trusted you." I didn't trust him, though.

In Patrick O'Brian's novels, Jack Aubrey and Stephen Maturin use a nautical metaphor for a blown chance: "He has missed his tide." To slip a frigate out of a narrow harbor you need a helping tide—but the tide doesn't wait. I began to accept that Day and I had missed our tide.

In eighth grade, Walker's feet grew lean and long, like scuba fins, and he shot up past Amanda. He was blithe and garrulous with his friends, but once their video chat was done, he clamped his Beats headphones tight—half-revealing his right ear for a moment if a parental remonstrance had to be logged and ignored. After considering his position in the family archipelago, he'd decamped a few islands away.

Addison, for her part, retired her cat's-ears headband without explanation, started teaching herself to play the ukulele, and announced that she was a vegetarian. After a few months of waking up hungry at 1:00 A.M. and scarfing Triscuits, she agreed to consume fish and—so she could keep eating my Arrabbiata—bacon. She billed herself as the world's first baco-pescatarian.

Then she grew obsessed with the K-pop group BTS. One night, wearing e-girl makeup, she brought her computer to the dinner table to show us the video of BTS's hit "Black Swan." As the band members performed a ballet in an empty theater, Addison glowed like their impresario.

"What's the song about?" I asked.

"It's about the difficulty of being them," she said. She googled the lyrics in translation, and I looked over her shoulder:

If you can't make my heart shake
How can I die once like this?

"It's probably better in the original Korean," I said— and instantly, as Addison ran off in tears, wished I hadn't. *Whatever your kids get excited about, encourage it.*

In 2004, Day came to Manhattan for a session of the Group: a cornerstone of Paul's process was bringing parents in to question them. Day looked uneasy as he scanned the circle, trying to figure out who was in charge. I felt anxious and numb.

When someone asked him about Mom, Day said, "She was controlling. *Charmingly* controlling, but extremely so." He told a story I'd never heard: when I was a toddler, Mom had angrily yanked me up from the floor, dislocating my shoulder. The doctor had to reset it. "Here was a man she could resent and he could not respond—a two-year-old child," Day said, feelingly.

Someone asked about the Swarthmore years. "I wish I could have been a decent college president and a great father," he said, "but I was an okay college president and a passable father." He added that he hadn't had a role model for any of it: "I do feel immeasurably better off as a father than as a son. And Tad and I can talk about what matters!" He looked over, and I nodded.

Paul smiled wolfishly and said, "We have seen Tad

growing in expressing himself emotionally, not just cere-
brally, in here. Have *you* noticed this growth?"

"I *have* noticed," Day said. "I don't *measure* it. I am glad
to talk with him about anything at any time."

We had dinner afterward, and I thanked him, knowing that he'd felt exposed and that he surely hated being
unable to tidy up the impressions he'd given. It was a quiet
meal. Day wrote an Indonesian friend to describe the session: "I was usefully revealing and candid, while main-
taining balance and proportion, and some dignity within
indignities. Tad seemed to appreciate it as useful, although
he admitted it was exhausting just listening. And I certainly felt drained by an hour and a half onstage before
8 bright thirty-something Manhattanites and their guru."
He concluded, "I am tempted to say that it is advanced sha-
manistic ritual, without resulting in the purifications possible through priesthood. Tad would answer, Socratically I
suppose, that self-knowledge is better than absolution. He
certainly seems confident and happy. But I would attribute
most of that to Amanda."

He told his analyst that he had misgivings about his
conduct, particularly about having revealed that Mom had
yanked me up: "Tad may overfix on it." His analyst, who
had also treated Mom, said, "The shoulder story bothered Elizabeth a good deal." It didn't upset me, though; I'd
always felt that Mom's ebullience about me was shadowed
by guilt.

His therapist's overall view, according to Day's notes,
was "Tad is afraid E. hampered his masculinity, and that
I didn't intercede enough for him." As result, the therapist
suggested, I identified with Mom and later "cast" Amanda

as Day in my internal drama. I was angry because I really wanted to be Day: "Tad fears he didn't choose the stronger parent." This diagnosis struck me as subtle, fascinating, and peculiar: Mom was always the stronger parent. I thought his therapist was on firmer ground when she told Day that the difficulties between us arose because "Tad wants you to be a different person. In his idealized father there is a way he wants you to be." She was trying to reassure him that my wishes weren't his responsibility. But I absolutely did want him to be different.

And so did he. A week later, he returned to Paul's office to watch the tape of his session. He found it "disenchanting." "OK, so I 'acquitted myself well.' But that tentativeness, that inerasable diffidence, those overshaded distinctions, that undershaded skull (that *baldness;* that Celtic flush; that simple Reaganesque *moue,* with crinkles at the corners of the eyes: that's me?) I would rather have come across as various; predictable-never; as spontaneous (even though rehearsed), as formidable, dauntless, gentle, modest, funny, infinite, sweet, and brave."

In 2018, I suddenly couldn't read the eye chart past the colossal E. My ophthalmologist said, "You've got a little yellow discoloration in both lenses. Because you're young for this I don't want to say 'cataracts,' but . . ." All that skiing and sunbathing as a boy. A year later, when I could barely decipher street signs, I got my cataracts cut out in West Orange, New Jersey. First the right eye and two weeks later the left, "Bohemian Rhapsody" blaring in the operating theater for both. Booyah, Dr. Rosenberg!

After the first procedure, I could half-see again. The

prismatic clarity of color! But in the mirror, my nearsighted eye picked out pimples among the wrinkles, and my far-sighted eye saw that the indignities of age don't replace the indignities of youth, they just pile on.

Grandma Jess, always wary and often sniffy, became in her eighties a surprising victim of Publishers Clearing House. She grew enraged when anyone tried to hint that she hadn't won the $10 million grand prize. Day wrote her a gently urgent letter on the topic—"Honest skepticism, I hope you understand, can be true love in these circumstances"—two weeks before her fifth and final heart attack.

Late credulity runs in the family. Day began falling for every scam going, from the *Who's Who in America* racket to the Western Union con. Whenever his phone rang it was someone who'd gotten his number from the dark web. He bought sheets of silver dollars from these hucksters, only to be bewildered when his purchases arrived. He'd always collected coins for their narratives—the rulers, trade routes, dreams of empire; when I was eight, he gave me a bag of copper farthings inscribed with Queen Victoria's image that he'd picked up in India. These new coins, vastly overpriced American Eagles and Peace Dollars, told only of his vulnerability.

He took the driving test that fall: forty-five minutes of cognitive questions and some navigating around a course in a parking lot. "I may have done OK on the cognitive," he wrote Timmie afterward. "But in the driving I was guilty of three faults in the judgment of Mary Ann, the tester. And her conclusion was that I should be advised *not* to drive. This is a great disappointment to me. I considered one of

my errors a serious misjudgment of spatial relations"—
he'd run over the cones—"but the other two noted by her
not serious, although she apparently found them so. I have
swallowed the bitter pill," he concluded, "but it will take
some time to digest it."

The Group got harder, and more valuable, once I started
leading with my feelings. I felt painfully self-conscious at
first, then gradually more comfortable, if not yet fully so.
But four years in, Paul began the session with a startling
announcement: he might have to shut us down, because
Sylvia had grown concerned about the Group's effect on our
individual therapies. The following week, he added that she
had accused him of hubris. The week after that, he flashed
a grin and said, *Never mind, all good.* Meanwhile, Sylvia
said that her concerns were entirely different. Mom and
Dad were fighting and they wouldn't tell us why. When
I pushed her, she alluded to Paul's "boundary violations"
with patients. I began to wonder about his need to bring our
parents in and tear them down, his need to be our paterfa-
milias.

A few weeks later, Paul dissolved the Group to preserve
his reputation with us—thereby destroying his reputation
with us. Once my anger cooled, I was surprised to realize
that I felt sorry for him. He'd have hated that.

After my eye surgeries, we all drove down to visit Day. A
storm had swept the air clean, and the damp, shimmering
light picked out pylons electric with current and trailers
suckling at the endless loading bays of Amazon, Prologis,
and Petco. The sunset was so crisp the eighteen-wheelers

appeared to burst into flames. When the Jersey Turnpike landscape catches your eye, the universe is telling you to pay attention.

Amanda and the kids went out to get groceries. Day was dozing on his four-post bed. "Taddio!" he called out. "How's the man?" I hugged him, gingerly, as he could no longer reciprocate. Sitting beside him, I announced that I'd just had my cataracts out.

"Cataracts!" His eyes popped open.

"Didn't you have them in both eyes, too?"

"Yes, they were removed fourteen years apart. So I know how you must feel about your restored vision." He traced the crown of his head with his fingertips, and added, "My left knee is paining me."

"Your severed ligaments?" At Swarthmore, he got steamrolled by a student in a pickup soccer game.

"Yes—from a red-card foul!" He glared around as if the culprit might be hiding nearby.

"Do you remember Ejaz Rahim?" I said. "The Eisenhower Fellow you put me in touch with in 1989, when I was traveling in Pakistan? When I was in his office in Peshawar, he asked about your knee, for some reason."

"Oh, yes, we had discussed it," he said airily, as if his knee was then a global topic. "What did *you* talk with him about?"

"Well, let's see," I said. Rahim, a mustachioed civil servant who wrote poetry, was in charge of the country's tribal area. He'd given me lunch, then provided me with an eight-soldier escort through the Khyber Pass into Afghanistan. It was a generous impulse, and perhaps a tutelary one—an edification in the harsh landscape where Western armies met their dooms. "I remember he said that in the tribal area there weren't any courts, so if you got into a dispute with someone, you kidnapped their close relative as a bargaining chip. If the village elders couldn't work out the dispute, then Ejaz had the power to replace them. He said it all tended to work out."

"It's a wise man who knows when to replace the elders," Day said. He fell heavily silent, his soaring brain pinioned by his landlocked body. I told him that between my surgeries I'd gotten shingles on my chest and arm, just as he once had. "Yes, on my belly," he said, perking up again. "Shingles is not a very philosophic disease."

"No—but what disease is?"

"Insanity," he said, and he laughed. His teeth were turfed about like old headstones.

"The pain of shingles can drive you kind of insane."

"We all get there in the end." Hearing a droning noise, he listened for a moment, then said, "Here come the bombers." His house is in a dell surrounded by woods, and planes climbing out from the Philadelphia airport, ten miles south, sound like B-1 bombers on the History Channel. Once the plane passed over, he grinned: still here. When his breathing began to slow, I kissed his forehead and told him I'd be in the next room. "So if I call 'Tad' you'll hear me?"

"Oh, yes. Try it in a minute and see."

"I will!"

But in a minute, he was asleep.

Ashes

SOME YEARS back, a man named Tyler Cassity, whom I was going to write about, began our first meeting by saying he'd looked up some of my stories: "You're fascinated by death, aren't you?" I temporized, taken aback, but he ticked off my recent topics: a mysterious dying boy; HBO's *Six Feet Under*; people who jump off the Golden Gate Bridge. That he was a cemetarian clinched his point.

Two years after I wrote about Cassity, I profiled the officer who oversaw the execution protocols at San Quentin Prison. I began to think of his unspoken horror of his job as the Shoeshine Problem. As a guard, not shining your shoes before you execute a prisoner would be unforgivably disrespectful—yet shining your shoes in order to execute him would be unforgivably punctilious. If there's no right answer about whether to shine your shoes, maybe the shoes aren't the problem.

In reporting on the jumpers at the Golden Gate, the world's leading suicide magnet, I learned that even those who seem determined to end their lives often long to be saved. As the suicidologist E. S. Shneidman observed, "The paradigm is the man who cuts his throat and cries for help in the same breath."

Death rarely comes when you're composed and ready.

It fell to me, as Day's eldest child and the one most accustomed to upsetting him, to ask him about his memorial service. It was the summer of 2019, and his infirmity had progressed. His internist, Dr. Karen Bowles, had told me that he had six months, maybe a year—and she'd said that six months earlier.

I found him in his study, bent over a cup of Irish Breakfast sugar. When I inquired how he'd like us to celebrate his life, when that time eventually came, he seemed surprisingly pleased. Later, I'd find a twenty-year-old file, "Death (My Own Astonishing) and Funeral (My Joyous)," that showed he'd given his send-off considerable thought. In it, he suggested that his funeral reflect "Japanese aesthetics/ Scots-Irish drinking habits," and include the Navy Hymn, "For Those in Peril on the Sea"—one of Mom's favorites— "because I never learned to swim."

Leaning back, chin in hand, the professor in office hours, Day said he'd like his ashes to lie in the columbarium at Bryn Mawr Presbyterian Church, where he'd interred Mom's. "I don't know if my ashes can be mixed with hers," he added, frowning.

"Would you want that if they could?"

A considering pause. "I don't think that's my deepest desire." As I took notes, I thought, not for the first time, *Why is she in there? She loved the Revolutionary War cem-*

etery in Woodstock where Grandma Tim is buried, the timo-
thy grass and drowsy afternoon shade.

"Do you have a niche reserved at the church?"

"Well, I don't recall," he said. "There's someone in charge of plots over there. 'Plots' in the sense of . . ." His fingers clutched at the air.

"Not stories but endings?"

He nodded.

Every Halloween, Amanda carved two pumpkins and I put them on the railing of our tiny deck, facing the kids' window. We lit tea candles inside them at night, so that Walker and Addison could see the jack-o'-lanterns shine as they fell asleep.

When they were two, one of the pumpkins rotted a few days after Halloween, so I blew out its candle and tossed it.

In the morning, Walker said, "Pumpkin gone away?"

"I put it in the trash." He looked terrified. "When pumpkins get old, they go in the trash." He began to cry. I said, "It's *normal*, Froggie."

"Addie get old, Addie in the trash?"

I tried to explain the difference between pumpkins and people, but he stayed close to his sister all day, watching me warily.

"Who would you like to have speak at your service?" I asked. Day named two eminent Southeast Asian historians. "Anyone else?"

He searched his memory. His funeral file contained a list of potential speakers, surprisingly including Eugene

Lang—"Because a critic is needed"—but by the time of our conversation almost all of them were dead except Donald Rumsfeld, who was dead to Day. He finally shrugged: no.

"Um, any friends or family?"

I could see him clambering, in his head, around the family tree. Its upper branches contain a few no-account senators; Lincoln's worst general-in-chief; and his great-grandfather, James Wood Friend, a robber baron whose wealth paralyzed his heirs until they rid themselves of it in the usual ways—indolence and drink, mostly. Day mentioned three older relatives. Then he grimaced: all dead.

In high school and college you're mewed up tight with your friends and then there's a big bang, the inflationary expansion of career and marriage and children, and everyone you knew is suddenly light-years distant. The hyperexpansion is unnoticeable, but one day the constellations are unfamiliar.

Will Schenck was a polestar through all that, a friend from when we were single and stupid together, who got married the same year Amanda and I did. I liked Will, I now realize, because he was the male, profane, excitable version of Mom. He was the sort of sandy-haired fellow you'd wonder about if you were paging through your yearbook—what's old Will up to? But in Will's case you'd know, because he kept in touch. "Buddy Boy!" his calls began. We both loved Billy Wilder's *The Apartment,* in which Jack Lemmon, climbing the greasy pole at an insurance company, is "Buddy Boy!" to the carousing execs he seeks to please. As Will climbed the greasy pole in ad sales at Condé Nast, he glad-handed widely, on the rolls of a half dozen clubs.

Though he often stepped in it during the membership interviews—"Do you go by 'Robert' or 'Bob'?" he'd ask a gatekeeper named Richard—he'd slide through on sheer longing. Amanda often remarked on Will's sweetness, his ingenuousness; at times he reminded me of the baby bird in *Are You My Mother?* who falls from the nest and wanders the world asking that question of every passing cow and steam shovel.

After a few years in AA, he convinced himself that he could drink socially. "Just put it on my tab!" he'd cry, swaggering among the rhino heads. His marriage seemed happy, and he had two great kids, but maturity never quite muted the noises in his head. A devoted fisherman, he had a glove box stuffed with speeding tickets acquired en route to the tranquilizing stream. He very nearly killed me and two other friends once, the cruise control on his dad's Saab pinned at ninety as he flew into a traffic jam—"I've got no brakes!"—because, in the unfamiliar vehicle, he was stamping the clutch. Yet his wide-eyed remorse compelled forgiveness.

Golf was what made Will a legend. He once birdied the first two holes at a tough Jack Nicklaus course and became convinced that he was finally going to break 80. Slowing to a dawdle, he took out his favorite four-wood to play it safe: the third hole had a canal all down the left. He took three meditative breaths and spaghettied his arms with his eyes closed, visualizing. Then he dribble-hooked his drive into the canal. Mastering his emotions, he reteed, repeated his routine at half his previous speed, and dribble-hooked his second ball into the canal. He flung his four-wood down the fairway—only he hooked it, too, so it flew even farther into the canal than his drives. "Oh, no!" he cried, and sank to his knees, helpless with laughter.

Every summer, a dozen of us, a shambolic troop of teachers, writers, and ad guys, held a four-round tournament in Saint Johnsbury, Vermont. We called ourselves the Monkeys because we gibbered like baboons, and we made the six-hour drive to stay at a dive motel and play thirty-six holes a day because baboons defend their territory. Will loved the Monkeys and was desperate to take home the winner's Green Jacket, a shapeless thrift-shop special invariably purchased in haste. Yet for a dozen years he was an also-ran. He was bedeviled by Saint J's fourteenth hole, which required a drive over a long gulch to a severely canted fairway; he'd often come to the hole playing well only to bury a couple of balls in the gulch. We all feared fourteen, but it was Will who named it the Ass-hole.

He joined Stanwich, an exclusive golf club in Connecticut, so he could practice every day and shave his handicap to the bone. On a cloudless morning that July, he double-bogeyed Saint J's first two holes. With seventy holes to go he was at most three shots behind, but he wailed, "I'm out of it already!"

One Saturday morning, in the spring of 2007, Day called as I was feeding the kids. He said that Pier and his wife, Sara, were visiting for the weekend, and observed that the day was balmy but not overhumid. Meteorology constituted much of his phone game, though we lived ninety miles apart and had the same weather.

Then he mentioned that Mary Petrie, who lived next door to our family's Wainscott house, had called that morning about Norah. Norah Pierson, Mom's sixty-six-year-old first cousin, oversaw the property. A jewelry maker who drove a lavender VW Bug festooned with "Peace" stickers, she teemed with conspiracy theories and was spikey as a horse chestnut, regularly bringing dinner conversation to a halt by barking something like "It's because we have a cunt!" She and I had had savage fights over minutiae— the seventy dollars she owed me for sea bass, say—but she was always touchingly repentant afterward. A few weeks earlier, she'd called to ask how the writing was going on *Cheerful Money,* and to declare that if any of our relatives took it amiss, "Fuck 'em! You're an artist!"

Day said that Norah had had a fierce migraine the previous afternoon, so Mary had gone to check on her that night, in her cottage across from the main house, and found her asleep. Checking again this morning, Mary had found her "non-responsive." As he recounted how she had called the police, and how an ambulance had come, I imagined, given his unhurried narrative, that Norah must be in the hospital. But, no, it finally emerged, she was dead.

When Mom was diagnosed with breast cancer, in 1995, it had spread to her lymph nodes. She opted for an experimental course of high-dose chemotherapy followed by a stem-cell transplant—a full reboot. Day quit EEF to take care of her, but after she got blasted by ten times the usual dose of Cytoxan and twenty times the usual dose of thiotepa, he seemed unable to express what was happening. "She has continuing debility and febrility," he said. "The nadir was on Wednesday night—symptoms not to be described." He sought refuge in euphemism and the passive voice, as he had when he told me about his own cancer: "The doctors discovered a carcinomic lesion of the prostate."

Mom explained that because all the fast-dividing cells in her body were under attack, her mouth and esophagus were coated with blisters that bled so much that for a week she couldn't speak, she could only gurgle; she vomited so profusely she wrenched her back; and she had constant diarrhea. Every inch of her was in agony. She said it was like being in a prison colony in French Guiana, except that in a prison colony you could choose to die. She'd never been to French Guiana, let alone sentenced to a prison colony there, but she had a knack for analogy.

Mom's spirit eventually bounced back, and she was newly grateful, even buoyant. When she and Day were brushing their teeth one night, he wrote me to report, she studied her bald head in the mirror, and said, "I look like a Martian."

Day said, "Really you look more like an actor made up for Noh drama."

Mom gave a soft scream and shook her head in the Japanese tremolo. "Do you love me?"

"Yes, I love you."

"Why?"

"Only three reasons. Because you are courageous, tender, and amusing."

She thought it over. "That's enough, I guess."

During her checkups, Mom carried Malta the bear into the CT scanner to assuage her claustrophobia. When the scans came back clean for five years, she felt she was cured. She'd beaten it. "Ta-da!" she cried, doing a few Charleston kicks in the general direction of French Guiana.

*   *   *

Day continued to mull family members who could elegize him. "Who could speak in place of my brother?" he said at last. "Nobody." Charles had died of lung cancer in 1994. They were never close, though they wanted to be.

"What about Ted Terry?" I asked, surprised Day hadn't already named his oldest friend, an acerbic trusts-and-estates lawyer. They always greeted each other boisterously, with their prep school nicknames: "Reen!" "Fritz, kid!" Day put Ted on the Eisenhower Exchange board, and Ted treated us to numberless rounds of golf—old boys old-boying in the traditional way. The golf outings were somewhat ticklish, though: Ted played hastily, always looking over his shoulder for waiting members, and Day spent an eternity over his shots, doing something complicated with his breathing, before taking a mighty lash that often laid sod over the ball.

"Yes . . ." he said. They hadn't seen each other in several years. It could just have been health and distance—Ted lived in Manhattan, and was hampered by Parkinson's—but I wondered whether there was more to it, some deeper inability to aid each other in the homestretch. "Ted won almost every argument we ever had, and we argued constantly. But I always felt he was arguing from the weaker, slipperier position." Day sipped some tea, then spread his hands in a pastoral gesture: *Ted could speak.* "A friendship of seventy years should be recognized. I do think his desire to be witty may get the better of him, though." He added, with the ghost of a grin, "Of course, there's no guarantee he'll outlive me."

In January 2003, Day jotted a note on a Post-it: "Nothing as important as love / Unless, of course, it be discernment."

Six months later, Mom's speech suddenly grew garbled, and scans revealed a gummy mass on her heart's mitral valve. I brought Malta to the hospital to keep her company. Antibiotics led to rapid improvement, and the doctors decided on a simple procedure to replace the valve. When I called her room the night before the operation, Timmie picked up and said that a rehabilitation therapist had taken Mom for a short walk. When she got back, I told her, "I hear you were running up and down the stairs like a mountain goat."

"Oh, yes," she said, "leaping from crag to crag!"

As they were rolling her off the next morning, she tucked her favorite bear into the breast pocket of her pajamas, so his head peeked out. A charm for the voyage. Somewhere in the flurry of prep, or the chaotic aftermath once Mom's heart stopped—the cancer had returned, everywhere—Malta disappeared.

They took us upstairs to see her. She was bound in a sheet, her mouth open as if in song. As a chaplain led us in the Lord's Prayer, Day began to sob. It was the only time I remember seeing him cry. When he got the call in 1976 that his father had died, he sat erect on the stool by the phone, taking notes as Mom rubbed his back.

That night, he asked, "Was that you, rubbing my back in the hospital room?" "Yes," I said. "I thought so," he said.

At Mom's interment, I read Canon Holland's famous assertion, a favorite of hers. It begins, "Death is nothing at all. It does not count. I have only slipped away into the next room," and ends, "I am but waiting for you, for an interval, somewhere very near, just round the corner. All is well. Nothing is hurt; nothing is lost. One brief moment and all

will be as it was before. How we shall laugh at the trouble
of parting when we meet again!"

This consolation soon proved itself inane, the brunch
music of solace. In the months after Mom's death, a great
joke or lasagna could rouse me to something near enjoy-
ment. But it was the structure of pleasure without the con-
tent, the husks.

Everyone said the season of grief would last a year.

Will Schenck finally won his Green Jacket in piratical style,
quit Stanwich in triumph—and promptly joined several
other clubs, still seeking that one place he'd feel at home.
The prostate cancer that overtook him several years later
was equally piratical, but if he had a moment of self-pity I
didn't see it. In March 2017, when he was thin as a rake, he
told me, "Without the cancer, I wouldn't have the clarity I
do now." He was going to Mexico to try the Gerson Therapy:
fruit juices and coffee enemas. He went on, "The cancer
saved me. I would never have found the peace I have today
if they hadn't had to—and this is highly confidential—cut
off my balls."

"Highly confidential," I repeated.

He began to laugh: "Oh, Buddy Boy!" Years earlier, I'd
asked where he'd met two of the Monkeys he'd brought
into the troop. "I can't really say because it's highly confidential," he'd said. "But we met in AA."

That May, after he came home to die, one of the Monkeys texted to suggest we all drive out for a visit. Will
replied that he wasn't up to it just yet, but added, "Don't
worry—I'm not out of it already, far from it. I'm going to

win this one. My love to the Monkeys. Tell those crazy bas-
tards I love them all."

On our next trip to Saint Johnsbury, we lined up across
the tee box at the fourteenth hole at sunset and drove balls
together into the gulch.

In the months after Mom's death, Day wrote dozens of
poems about her, including one about how he hoped to mix
their ashes:

> *Think well on this, my sweet:*
> *Our bodies need not truly beat*
> *Upon each other,*
> *But, past their funerary heat,*
> *Will slide together perfectly,*
> *Grain and micrograin*
> *Intimate and without stain,*
> *Closer than ever they were in life*

Free of her now, free of all those inaccessible grottoes,
Day was desolate. His analyst warned him not to woman-
ize: "You identify with your mother and you seek revenge
against her for the humiliation she caused your father.
Together they made a powerful combo—you must be on
watch against it."

In 2002, as he was finishing his Indonesia book, he'd con-
tacted Siti Z after several decades to tell her he planned to
write about her. When she seemed unruffled, he wrote, "It
relieves me to think that my book may not offend you. . . .
That you will forgive the injustice to you of my treating

our affinity as if it were only anthropology. We both know how much more it was." In a later letter, he added, "I convince myself that in writing my love for you, I love myself better, and love my wife more easily and fully. Is that self-deception? Or just possibly a simple syllogism of the spirit that I am late to discover."

His manuscript hinted at a liaison. When I read it and offered suggestions, I told him that that passage would be hard reading for Mom. It had been hard for me, this intimation of a secret life. He nodded slowly, his face careful— *How much to tell me of what Mom already knew? How much to tell me, in general?* Then he trimmed the passage considerably, to "She was compact, vigorous, prim. I found her alluring." *Indonesian Destinies* got the best reviews of Day's career—raves in the *Times* and *The Wall Street Journal;* raves everywhere, really. I was thrilled that his lifework had been recognized, and relieved, too: somehow it eased the pressure on both of us. But the book came out two weeks before Mom died.

A few months later, he went to Java on a promotional tour, and met Siti Z again. She promptly proposed again. He wrote her to pump the brakes: "From the beginning, however, I have told you about the depth of my love for Elizabeth. Her life is ended. But my love has not. I still feel married to her. She has been the chief shaping force in my life since we fell in love forty-five years ago."

My best guess is that the approach of death is like being on a plane that has crossed an ocean and is descending into dense fog. The view vanishes as rain beads on the window and the wind boxes the compass. Soon it's unclear which way is up. As you cinch your seatbelt tighter, your thoughts turn to the pilot: *Who is he? Does he know what he's doing? What do the instruments say?* This has happened billions of times, yet the question is always fresh and urgent: *Will I touch down at last in the desired city, welcomed over the intercom by a reassuring voice? Or, as I'm already invisible to everyone else, will I just disappear?*

In 2018, the Squash Nationals were in Philadelphia, and Day came to the courts to see me play Will Carlin. Slow to get into his caregiver Sam's car and slower to get out of it, he arrived midway through, wearing three fleeces and a hat large enough to advertise a taco chain.

Will and I were having our usual battle. I won the first game easily and had a game ball in the second. After some scrambly back-and-forth, I picked off a volley and put it away. Will, stuck behind me, asked for a let. I thought the ref's "No let" was correct, but Will was visibly upset, so I reversed the call. He ended up winning the game. But in the fourth, when the ref said "No let" on a ball I was convinced I'd have reached, Will granted me a let with a wry smile. I came back to win that game, 11–9, and Day, his chin on his cane, gave me a smiling thumbs-up.

At 6–6 in the fifth, Will hit a terrific series of low kills to run the game out 11–7. Day leaned down to say, "That was quite a match, you two," the lenses in his eyes glinting under the lights.

In the locker room, I began to ice my left knee, which ached now after hard matches. Ned Monaghan sat beside me and said, "Well fought, Tad." A mordantly cheerful Irishman who used to play with Day, Ned was a strong player in the seventy-plus bracket. "Do you know 'The Hurley Player'?"

"I don't think I do." I knew only that hurling was an Irish sport like field hockey.

He tugged his sweatpants to get comfortable. "It's by Winifred Letts, and oh, you must listen," he said. He began in a clarion voice:

> *"When you are old," she said, "grown old and grey ..."*
> *I laughed to hear her say it, till the cold,*
> *Strange thought came afterwards, you will be old*
> *Sometime and give your hurley stick away*
> *For someone else to play.*

The men nearby were listening, halfway out of their shorts or wrapped in towels. The whole room had fallen silent by the time Ned, beating time softly on his knee, wound up:

> *How will they know how strong you were and fleet,*
> *You who were once a storm wind and a flame?*
> *They will forget your fame*
>
> *They will not dream, these careless and uncouth,*
> *That you, who wag an old man's tedious tongue,*
> *Were once a splendour, tawny-haired and young*
> *But I shall laugh at them who doubt the truth*
> *Of your immortal youth.*

*   *   *

Putting my memorial service notes aside, I asked Day, "What's the worst thing about this phase of life?"

"The physical aspect," he said. "My knees are paining me." He began massaging them.

"I didn't know it was both knees now."

"Both knees don't hurt!" he yelled, waving at everything. Confidingly, he added, "But if I massage them beforehand, they might not hurt later."

"So it's precautionary." He nodded. "And the best thing?" He closed his eyes, drifting off. "If any."

He wagged his head, not to be rushed. "I have time to contemplate people and reconsider them," he said. A smile spread over his face.

"Oh?" *Maybe he was just saving his sweetness up for us till the end. The way we always hoped.* "Anyone in particular?"

"Well," he said, "I might be just about ready to change my mind about Franklin Roosevelt."

Every August, Amanda and I bike with the kids down the road to Wainscott Cemetery, where Norah is buried. It's a small graveyard dating from the eighteenth century: headstones downy with lichen, loosely interlaced family trees— Hedges, Talmage, Osborn—reconstellated in marble.

Norah's stone is simple, just her name and her dates. The kids, born the year before she died, don't recall her holding them when they were a month old, her beaming tenderness. So we lay our bikes down and talk about her. It always makes me wonder how they'll remember us.

Walker and Addison hop the rail fence and climb into the

open windows of a cabin on the playground next door. They crouch there, framed, larger every year, until we're ready to take the photo. Then they jump up and out together, so we can catch them at the apex of their flight.

Meanwhile

WHEN I lived with Melanie, in the early nineties, I was a bad boyfriend. In our four years together, I cheated on her with four women. I told myself that I was just confirming my misgivings. That was how Amanda understood these infidelities when I wrote about them in *Cheerful Money:* wild oats, a starter relationship, yada yada yada. She saw them that way because I hadn't told her that I had trouble with intimacy. It wasn't that I feared it—I longed for it. But I hated the idea of opening up and then being rejected, and I didn't trust anyone's promises of commitment. So I'd stress-test their sincerity. It was when Melanie was at her most vulnerable and trusting, when she'd just written me a loving note in her back-slanting cursive, that I would cheat.

I didn't tell Sylvia about this failing, and I didn't tell Paul and the Group, either. I was afraid that my inhibition disqualified me from being a bona fide human being, the kind with skin in the game. Paul once mentioned a patient who'd defended his infidelities by saying, "How is it hurting my wife, if she doesn't know?" "Because *you* know," Paul had replied. I logged that exchange, taking Paul's point—but secretly reserving judgment.

As a further safeguard, I tried to keep my problem hidden even from myself. Like the chicken pox I'd had at four, it lurked in my spine.

In 2004, Day began dating Mary. They argued a lot and laughed a lot, too. She inspired him to throw dinner parties and take bike trips and start living again. He made it clear to her, though, that he didn't intend to remarry. The following year, he plunged into an affair with a woman I'll call Leyla. He'd mentioned her to us, in a Billy Grassie sort of way, but in his journals he described their meetings in raunchy detail, calling it "the most daring and compelling ecstasy of my life." Thirty years his junior, she was married and had children. When she suggested that they marry, he roughed out an equation. Estimating the likelihood that she'd be able to "divorce without hatred" from her husband and children at .7, and that of "remarriage with easy understanding by my children, etc." at .21, he reckoned the "combined chances of success, family happiness, + personal happiness = much < than 1 percent."

Sex wasn't enough, he reminded himself: "I would feel like a game trophy as her husband, drilled through the heart and mounted, inert, for display. I would enter my eighties as she entered her fifties, with affairs still before her and debilities facing me. Ghastly scenario." Over tea in his kitchen, he broke it off, telling her, "Please go now, or I'll break down and weep." Leyla called him "harsh." Three weeks earlier, when he definitively rejected Siti Z's proposal, she had called him "heartless." His lovers were "unaware of each other," he wrote ruefully, "but converging in recriminations."

In 2007, he drafted a personal ad for *The New York Review of Books:* "Widower, happily married more than four decades, now surprised Jungian analyst describes him as 'erotic seeker.' Novelist, journalist, nationally ranked racquetsman looking for a finder-keeper. Never smoked; sometimes swears. Overtravelled but unweary; religious but underobservant; articulate mixed with taciturn. Would correspondence be a good way to begin? Simpleton@prodigy .net." He never ran the ad, but in 2008 he had a fling with Cho, the woman he'd hooked up with after his prostate surgery, twenty years earlier.

Day kept these intrigues from us, wanting to preserve our admiration. But when he wrote Cho to sever their tie, he told her that he didn't feel very admirable: "Whatever you say about me in your generosity, I am aging, fickle, frail, and foolish. I preach trust and violate it. I've practiced institution building, and now hoard myself in a private cell. Having been a passable president, I am now a failed hermit." He told me that it was in 2008, at seventy-seven, that he first felt old.

Privately, he did the math on his affairs: "Three women, at most five nights, in a marriage of forty-three years. It seems to me like minimal infidelity, given my mother's record in twenty-three years of being wed to my father. My behavior does not make me proud," he added, acknowledging that he'd been unfaithful to Mary, too. "But it seems inescapable because of the shape of the relationship between my mother and father. I seem to be the prisoner of my history, regrettable as that may be."

If you'd asked me, back then, I'd have guessed that Day had cheated on Mom. It just seemed intuitively likely. I sometimes think about his saying that he'd always trusted me—it feels like he *wanted* to, but that he couldn't, not quite. He recognized our congruence well before I did.

I cheated on Amanda in 2008, a few months after she'd read *Cheerful Money* and I'd assured her she had nothing to worry about. We'd survived the exhausted squabbles of the toddler period, and she was busy with her first start-up, Seawinkle. She would search my eyes at breakfast and confide her worries about her site's skeletal technology, trusting that we were fully in it together: the feedings and the changings and the sharing and the making-do. I could feel an ache rising in my throat; here was intimacy, at last. But I was afraid of the consequences if she knew how tightly my mood was tethered to hers, of how much I depended on her. I wasn't averse to committing to her completely—I was averse to committing to her completely at the price of being understood. Because if she really knew me, she'd realize she'd made a mistake.

I see that now. What I saw at a party in Los Angeles was a woman in a cocktail dress. She had a quizzical, slightly apprehensive look that I recognized from the mirror, and she laughed at my banter. Getting laughs was a drug for me—it certified that I was having an impact. We didn't have sex, but we came close. My emails home that weekend were as bare as rebar; I was appalled by myself, stunned. My betrayal was doubly painful: horrific on its own, and even more horrific because it left me so horrified by myself. Having long feared being known, I had cheated and lied in ways that gave credence to the fear.

I vowed it would never happen again. I'd had too much to drink, obviously, right? I don't drink much, usually, a beer at dinner. So four or five beers had made flirting a peripheral matter, numbing my awareness of imminent catastrophe. It had allowed me to act like a small child who pushes a glass off a counter—then jumps back and averts his gaze from the smithereens. *It smashed itself!*

But it wasn't the drinking that led to the cheating. It was the inhibition and the desire for attention—for a shallow kind of attention uncoupled to any deeper responsibility—that led to the drinking. I had given myself an excuse.

A few years in, Amanda and I realized that everyone at our table at our wedding had broken up. The beautifully dressed couple first: during one fight, he made her get out of their car and walk more than a mile home, carrying their baby. Then the barefoot-seeming couple: he'd had an affair because she wouldn't sleep with him. Then the artistic couple: he'd begun an affair because she was having one, or maybe vice versa. Then the final husband died.

Around 2010, our daily life started to feel chippy. Amanda's frolicking had subsided. Had I stifled it? I'd bristle at her jabs or respond in kind—"I *do* know what a salad spinner is!"—and she'd say, "That was a *joke*." It never sounded like a joke, though. When I'd say, "You should exercise more/sleep more/work less," she felt I wasn't trying to be helpful so much as booing from the sidelines. I was clearly getting old and cranky, like my dad. (I was forty-seven.)

We weren't having sex as much, either. It had never been the backbone of our relationship, and I was reluctant if Amanda wanted to make love on the beach or in the morning, when I felt groggy and in need of coffee. Without ever planning to or talking about it with her or trying to work on it together, I began to disengage. I would not allow her to get too close. She decided that I was just getting old and losing my pep, like my dad. And she was getting home tired from work, anyway, so . . .

There were plenty of warm, cozy days when we'd make pasta or bring home flowers from the stand by the subway, days of snuggling with Addison and Walker, so we had faith that our love was still there, under the pile of bills. I still perked up when I heard her approaching—that light, firm step, purposeful as a drum majorette. But when we bickered now it felt harsher. As we scarfed bowls of cereal one morning, with funding for the company's seed round yet again in doubt, Amanda declared, "I'd rather move to Siberia and live off the frozen tundra than accept defeat!" She dreaded ending up in a state-run nursing home and was angry that I wasn't reinventing myself to prevent that. Aside from going to visit relatives, we hadn't taken a vacation in years, because we couldn't afford to go anywhere. Surprise bills—*Oh, fuck, the kids also need textbooks!*—would send me into a panic of figuring out who we could stiff until the next paycheck cleared. This was normal life in freelance-world New York; a lot of our friends were ice cubes like us, riding on their own melting. But I was beginning to realize that our burn rate would eventually price us out of the city. Still, I was aggrieved that Amanda wanted me to change as fast as she was, so I hotly pointed out that she was not yet forty, and that I was working hard at a job that I loved and that was underwriting her ability to fight on. We were both mad at each other for not making more.

Amanda just wanted me to be kinder, gamer, more flexible. And I just wanted an apology—even one. She feared that if she apologized, I'd declare victory and desert the field. But it felt like she was withdrawing her hope, switching off her empathy, the way a freezing body retracts its blood to the torso. Or was that me? She dreaded bringing up thorny topics such as how we'd pay for Walker's and Addison's college education, because my cross-examinations would blow her backwards. It was hard to argue with her because she didn't always listen, and it was hard to argue with me because I always did: I listened for the flaws in her logic. I was fighting not to regain her admiration or to find a better way forward, but to prove her wrong. Asperity had become second nature. So she began to develop a carapace, to inure herself, and I began to lose hope that our love would grow. I started to play defense, just trying to get through it, whatever it turned out to be: the toddler years, the mortgage years, the remaining years.

After breakfast, we washed up in silence and trudged off to work. *Have a great day, honey! I'll drop you at that nursing home later!*

Feeling by turns crowded and abandoned, I convinced myself that I needed someone who'd recognize my shining qualities, if only for an hour or two. I was trying to get out of the fight, when marriage is all about staying in it. I asked an old friend to lunch because I liked the way she cocked her head when I spoke. Then we met for drinks, and then we made out a few times. I broke it off before it went any further: we lived in the same city, and it felt too close to Amanda and our marriage. Stuck in my scratchy groove, however, I kissed another married woman a few months later. It was quickly clear that we were just seeking distraction: she from boredom, and I from my growing awareness that I was stuck. Maybe the word is broken.

I didn't feel that my infidelities made me take any less joy in our children or in my writing or even in Amanda. I did fear—an occasional stab—that by constructing a safe room at the heart of my life, I was reducing the square footage available for everything else. And I sensed that by raising none of my fears and failures with Amanda I was building an airtight compartment for her, too. In a marriage, there are either no boxes or two boxes.

To the extent that I faced what I was doing, my murky expectation was that anything truly ruinous would happen outside the metropolitan area, geographically and emotionally remote from us. In some far-off city, where Life360's precision would raise no alarms if Amanda checked it—which she never did, because she trusted me. But I didn't want to be trustworthy. I wanted sympathy and admiration. Loyal to my loneliness, I saw my wounds as dueling scars. Without them, I'd be ordinary, and I was determined to be extraordinary. An outlier.

In 2011, I ran into Phyllis, a friend of a friend, at a restaurant in Los Angeles. I hadn't seen her in a decade or so, and she seemed pleased to stop and chat. We had a drink after lunch, then another. She was having troubles in her marriage and her career, and I was a good audience for tales of woe. I stood in the restaurant bathroom two hours later, urinating into a bed of crushed ice, the sun angling through the high window—that heart-stopping late-afternoon L.A. light—thinking, *This is a bad idea.*

But another, cozening voice reassured me, *It's Euro-*

*pean, worldly, inevitable: humans are not a faithful species.
Amanda will never have to know.* An hour later, I watched
my key card pass over the lock of my hotel room.

But I know.

I'd written a cryptic note of remorse in my journal after
my first infidelity, in 2008. Now I wrote about having had
a "boozy reunion" with Phyllis. The idea, I guess, was that
this code would defeat a casual reader. But there are no
casual readers of other people's journals.

I had a one-night stand in 2012 in another distant city, with
a woman who was a consultant, I think. We didn't talk about
her work. We didn't talk about anything, really. We had nothing in common except an itch—for sex, but really for attention. For a booster shot of self-esteem. The women weren't
particularly similar in temperament or appearance; what
united them was that they responded to me, that they saw
me. Only it wasn't really me they were seeing. Like a paranoid
autocrat, I had enlisted a body double to play me in public.

By working untold hours to get Food52 off the ground,
Amanda was finally able to pay herself $50,000 a year, then
$100,000. After years of blithely continuing to travel for
The New Yorker in my accustomed way, I finally recognized
that I needed to get moving, too. I began ghostwriting books
at night and on the weekends, doubling my income, and our
financial cramp began to recede.

But five years of privation were followed, biblically, by
five years of plagues that drove us nearly mad. After we
finally killed off our clothing moths, rats snuck in through
the building's basement at the same time that squirrels
began nesting in the eaves of the apartment upstairs. One

squirrel got stuck in our pocket door and another lay down and died at the foot of our bed. At night the rodent legions fought in the walls, gnawing and clawing and gnashing and squealing as we lay awake in despair.

We couldn't afford to move out as we laboriously patched the holes, rusticated the squirrels, and poisoned the rats. I came to loathe the stench of dead rat in the walls, which even the lavender candles we burned all day couldn't disguise. Shortly after the greasy black blowflies that had fed on the rats finally stopped buzzing around the kitchen, we got bedbugs. Then the moths returned. More of our clothing was being bug-bombed in plastic bags than was available to wear, and we didn't dare probe the dark corners for fear of discovering another two-thousand-dollar problem.

Throughout all this, we prided ourselves on being a good team. We tag-teamed the chores, threw fun dinner parties, and were raising delightful children. On Father's Day and my birthday and at Christmas, Amanda would write me immensely touching notes that detailed my best qualities, portraying me as "the strong, wise, thoughtful protector" or the "dependable and lovely anchor" that "all the tiny fishes and plants and people gravitate toward." I treasured how she saw me. "It's been so lovely," she wrote. "And is even when it doesn't seem to be."

Feeling "scorched, but strangely blessed" after his riot of carnality, Day focused on Mary and began a relaxed late flowering. I didn't really notice. Walker and Addison were keeping us busy in their preschool years, and Day never broadcast his contentment. Instead, he devised a family quiz that contained playful questions such as:

Which of these is your chief candidate for extermination
or abolition?

a. mosquito
b. capital punishment
c. Osama bin Laden
d. television
e. rat
f. other

And, while traveling in Turkey, he wrote:

Please assure my children
That before I died
I learned the words for please and thank you,
For excellent, and rice pudding.
And that I carry their own names
In my mind all the time,
And the thought of their mother,
And their dear small children, with love.

In 2011, he wrote in his journal, "Waking up on this
Father's Day in the year I turn eighty, I fault myself for
the rigidities and failures and emotional stinginesses that
my three children may feel or have felt in me. I hope they
phone, but it is unlikely that all three will do so. I want to
be forgiven, to be understood as the best I could make of
myself emotionally out of an early-foundered and falsely
sustained parental marriage. But I cannot expect that. I can
only forgive myself."

Yet serenity by the koi pond was not to be Day's denoue-
ment. He began importuning strangers, writing Amartya

Sen: Can I teach at your university? And Ralph Nader: What should I do with the rest of my life? And a younger woman he'd met at a dinner party: "No one before you has, in the course of a few hours and of glancing encounters in public, burned upon me such a fierce afterimage. My desire to embrace you emerges early in our conversation. Not yet to kiss you." After Mary downshifted their relationship, Day asked his doctor for Cialis and began making lunch dates with a new crush. But he went into the hospital again and forgot her name.

I saw Phyllis in L.A. every so often. Later in 2011, and once or twice the following year. We didn't sleep together then, though we kissed; she said she was working on her marriage. She'd occasionally ask whether I'd cheated with anyone else, and I'd always say "No." I lied though it was clear she didn't believe me, though there was no point to it. Mistrust had become my baseline state. When I emailed that I was coming to L.A., she began to ignore the message, or say she was busy. We slept together again a couple of years later, then she stopped responding again. She emailed me out of the blue and we hooked up one more time. After that, she went totally dark.

I kept trying to attract her attention the same way I'd kept trying to attract Natalie's, decades before. Beckoned, after some time with my air hose, I'd warily advance. Rebuffed again, I'd retreat, but watchfully. You can never get enough of what you do not really want.

Ripples

YOU ARE a flat stone. You begin to skip across the lake, generating ripples. Because of the uncertain nature of fluid dynamics, once eddies have been created, a skipping stone could theoretically, once in a great while, cause the lake itself to explode.

When I was young, I admired no writer's stories more than John Updike's. I became friends with a guy named Chris mostly because we both loved the opening run of "A Sense of Shelter":

> Snow fell against the high school all day, wet big-flaked snow that did not accumulate well. Sharpening two pencils, William looked down on a parking lot that was a blackboard in reverse; car tires had cut smooth arcs of black into the white, and wherever a school bus had backed around, it had left an autocratic signature of two Vs.

Book jackets sporting Updike's woodsy tousle and horndog smile were everywhere, like portraits of a Balkans despot. He surrounded us; in some thermostatic way he established the climate. I was already a watchful white guy and I already wrote for *The Harvard Lampoon,* as he had. All I had to do was move to New York, work at *The New Yorker,* sum up the culture, and reap the hosannas. Easy-peasy.

When I got to New York, burning with the prescribed low steady fever, I met with a *New Yorker* writer who'd been hired out of Harvard three years earlier, another Updike in utero. I'd sent him my clips, hoping he'd say, "You should start here tomorrow!" Scratching his ear meditatively, he in fact said, "You know what I'd do if I were you? I'd move to a place like Phoenix and write for an alternative newspaper. Learn how power shapes a midsized American city, and how to report, and all the facets of our craft. And *then,* after ten years or so, if you still have a mind to, return to New York."

I didn't move to Phoenix. But I also didn't punch him in the face.

A few years ago, for a BBC special about Adele, the network hosted an audition for Adele impersonators—with the singer herself competing as "Jenny," disguised by a prosthetic nose and chin. After a florid display of stage fright, Jenny launched into "Make You Feel My Love." As her vibrato shook the hall, the other eight impersonators began to catch on.

In the footage the BBC used, the almost Adeles seemed thrilled that their exemplar was among them. But I found the stunt unbearably cruel. What was she establishing, other than that even her most devoted students couldn't come close? Great artists are perforce unwittingly cruel to the rest of us, but why say the quiet part out loud?

In the early eighties, Day began work on an autobiographical novel about a young man's privileged boyhood in Pittsburgh. In 1983, he wrote, "What I aim to achieve in my first novel: a thing of beauty, terror, and tenderness. I hope that in its way, to the fullest extent of my limited power, the novel can inspire, chasten, and give joy." The following year, when he was deeper into the book, he declared that as a novelist "I am first a humanist, next an urban anthropologist, and only third an artist. I cannot aspire higher, say, than the level of Galsworthy. That allows me to admire Thomas Hardy, without trying to compete with him."

In high school, he wrote a short story about a boy who sees his mother kissing Santa Claus. His parents sat him down and Grandpa Ted said, "We don't talk about those things." Day would later recall that "I obeyed, and wrote no more such stories. But it did seem, however limited was my talent, that their requirement of me was an offense against artistic truth." He once told me he'd spent much of his life documenting American imperialism because "nobody in the family had ever told me any family history. So I decided, I'm going to write a history that Americans don't know and may not want told." *Family Laundry* was the history his family had not wanted told: the narrator, Randall McCalla, pores through newspaper archives to get to the bottom of an ancient scandal in which an adventuress bilked his great-grandfather of $800,000—a scandal that, in real life, had ensnared James Wood Friend. Randy also unearths his mother's infidelities and his drunken father's fatal passivity.

A few drafts in, I convinced Day to shift from the third person to the first, as it was so plainly his story (I suspect he named his narrator "Randy" in tribute to his own libido). A writer of memoirs or bildungsromans is usually an insider who feels like an outsider. A writer who's comfortable code-switching between those modes, as Day and I are, will likely be drawn to secrets: unearthing them—and also keeping them. *Family Laundry* reminded me of *All the King's Men,* in which the narrator investigates his father, fearing that he'll find something unsavory, and does. Randy's feelings made painful reading:

> I admit that I did not love my father as much as I should have. How much was that? More than I did anyway. How much could I have loved him? Infinitely more. Oh, sure, I answer myself, but you are not a saint, and your capacities are strictly finite, and maybe your ability to love is meagre, whatever the reasons. *Meagre.* There's a self-judgment that freezes me in my footsteps.

Yet the book struck me as a historian's novel, one animated less by emotional imperatives than by cultural tides. After the main female character commits suicide, Randy blames it on the punitive aspects of Calvinism and winner-take-all capitalism: "I am offering the notion that Barbara Quick is the victim of bad Protestant theology from the sixteenth century and impossible social teleology from the twentieth. . . . She was caught between an overly cruel notion of the divine and an excessively optimistic view of American opportunity."

When *Family Laundry* was published, in 1986, review-
ers were more generous (The *Times* wrote that "Mr.
Friend has conducted a difficult inquiry with energy, sensitivity and determination"). After reading his appraisals,
Day smilingly told me, "I think it possible, with a few
more novels, that I may carve out a minor place in American letters."

Day at Pier's wedding.

Early on in New York, I took a photography class, trying out
a new way of seeing. I bought a used Canon and set off on my
first assignment: shoot a roll in your neighborhood. I walked
around the West Village peering through the viewfinder,
and finally framed up a peach-brick wall stenciled with a
feedlot ad: the nineteenth-century city, persisting still.

As I clicked the shutter, someone tapped my shoulder. A
very short, very old woman swathed in black peered up at
me, waiting until I lowered the camera. "I was a friend of

Walker Evans's," she said. "You know Walker Evans, the photographer?"

"Of course," I said, preparing to be delighted. She was about to share an Evans tip or compliment my eye. Or both!

"He would *never* have taken that photograph."

Mom loved telling the story of how, as a sophomore at Smith College, she'd placed second to Sylvia Plath in a poetry contest judged by W. H. Auden. She'd end it by tossing her head and declaring it was just as well she hadn't won: "Head in the oven, and so forth!" In the early years of her marriage she maintained a recipe box of notes and poems filed alphabetically under themes such as "Age," "Betrayal," "Men Who Didn't Get To Be Presidents," and "Perfection and then what?" Her poetry, she declared, "confronted the misery in the world."

When she turned to painting, in her forties, her canvases were bright and buoyant. They celebrated Molly napping, sunlight slanting through a mullioned window, the intricate pattern of a Spode teacup. Aside from her tempera study of Day in his bathrobe, only one picture confronted the ambient misery: her last big work, after her chemo, a bleak self-portrait in which she was surrounded by sinister mythical animals. None of us liked it, which Mom took as confirmation that we only loved her when she set out to charm. But if you hide your true self for decades, you can't in fairness complain about being misunderstood—unless you're a member of my family.

Addison showed an early aptitude for verbal compression. At eight, she wrote a poem for my birthday:

The great apple
Tree shakes as
The wind blows
And fallen wishes
Are taken into
The wild and
Lovely world.

At breakfast, a few months later, she told me, "Daddy, I think I want to be a poet!"

"That's great, sweetie!" I said. "You have a gift for putting your feelings into words." Behind her, Amanda was vigorously shaking her head. "Of course," I went on, "you also have to figure out a way to support yourself. A poet named Robert Graves once observed, 'There's no money in poetry.'" Bending close, I whispered, "He added, 'But then there's no poetry in money, either.'"

Amanda worried that I'd pass on my Waspy expectation that some maiden aunt's bequest would always turn up to tide us over. My faith in muddling through did seem crazy when I thought about it, so I tried not to think about it.

From the late eighties to the mid-nineties, I did most of my writing for *Esquire*, *Vogue*, and *New York*, supplying snark and occasional heft to magazines whose ideal cover line was THE SPICE GIRLS IN THE SPICE ISLANDS. A number of people told me I should write fiction. I was never sure whether this was a compliment or a suggestion that I had missed my tide.

I was fiction-adjacent, fiction-curious. When a Hollywood agent said, of a female CEO, "I've never seen so much cleavage on an intellectual!" it illuminated a potential novel for me—but dimly, as in a séance. I could imagine the bumptious agent, but not his world. Likewise, the master publicist who declared, after the police denied him a permit for a lavish stunt, "It's a sad day for American capitalism when a man can't fly a midget on a kite over Central Park." I set these skeleton keys in a notebook, then set the notebook aside.

Fiction seemed both too naked and too exalted. I was paralyzed by a youthful belief that there was a greatest sentence ever, early in Faulkner's *The Wild Palms:* "It was overcast; the invisible wind blew strong and steady among the invisible palms, from the invisible sea—a harsh steady sound full of the murmur of surf on the outside barrier islands, the spits and scars of sand bastioned with tossing and shabby pines." Now, I don't know. It's a tremendous sentence: the breasting clauses, the repetitions and alliterations pulsing like the invisible wind itself. But its magic has faded some as I've learned the trick of it. Writing isn't about sentences; any number of people can write a nifty sentence. The writers who came to grip me—Shirley Hazzard, Cormac McCarthy, Alice Munro—were wizards with structure who didn't flinch from their characters' dooms.

I'm still partial to Faulkner's use of the em dash—which permits further specification or the introduction of a counterforce, an undertow—and the semicolon; I believe in independent clauses, twin pathways that diverge. Donald Barthelme, Kurt Vonnegut, and James Salter weren't wrong to strip semicolons from their own work; they were wrong to prescriptively abhor them. Syntax is style, and style is a writer's mode of apprehension.

In 1957, after two brilliant years in Manhattan, John Updike moved to Ipswich, Massachusetts. Years later, he explained: "I went to a party at Brendan Gill's in Bronxville and it was full of these people I revered—Robert Coates, Janet Flanner, Gill himself; old *New Yorker* hands, people who had poured their creativity into the magazine—and they struck me as very sad; I'm not sure why. They all drank. I came home from that party and I said to my wife—in my memory, at least, my fabulizing memory—I said, 'Let's get out of here.'"

* * *

Day was a year behind A. R. Gurney at Saint Paul's and Williams and then played squash with him in Buffalo. Gurney came late to his purpose—the precondition for candor being his father's death—and then produced such lacerating work as *The Dining Room* and *The Cocktail Hour*. Yet Day never thought of his friend as a writer worth venerating. How could anyone you grew up with be an artist? Artists inhabit remote cabins or Russian cemeteries. I found this position ridiculous—even Prince lived next door to *somebody*—yet oddly persuasive.

Day also felt that I was slumming. When I appeared on *The Charlie Rose Show*, talking with three other writers about feminism and sex (a topic I'd just written about for *Esquire*), he was nonplussed. "What was the value added for American culture?" he wrote me to inquire. "I wonder if the transcript of the whole hour would contain a single utterance of the world 'love'? The program should rather have asked, 'What makes love sometimes descend into rage?'; or, 'What are the ways that anger may be authentically part of love; may co-exist non-destructively with love, or may be subordinated into love?' "

In 1998, a dozen years later than the Updike Protocol had prescribed, I joined the staff of *The New Yorker*. One of my first stories was about two workmen in Sun Valley who'd dug up a jar of gold coins on land owned by the *Rolling Stone* founder Jann Wenner; each schemed to take the treasure for himself, but Wenner ended up with it. Day wrote, "It may be rather nineteenth century of me, but I wondered what *The New Yorker*'s goal was in publishing it. To show the triumph of a New Yorker who didn't care?"

After I stopped responding to these irksome questions, he stopped posing them.

He was always more appreciative after the fact, once you'd entered history. When A. R. Gurney died, in 2017, Day wrote his widow, "My sense of loss is nothing compared with what I imagine you now feel. Your loss is surely great. But America's quiet pain has been even greater."

When the kids were nine, we took them on their first trip abroad: a week in Panama. The canal was gigantic; everything else was modest and charming. I snapped a photo of Walker and Addison being licked by just-born baby goats. Walker's hands are under his chin and his face is tilted up in absolute delight.

No one thinks of Panama as the pinnacle of anything, not even Panamanians. They bill their waterway as the world's second-most-famous canal, after the Suez; their Geisha as the world's second-tastiest coffee, after Yirgacheffe; and their quetzal as the world's second-most-beautiful bird, after the peacock. But I love that kind of Avisland because you can meet its expectations. As Walker declared while we were gliding down the canal, "If I had to be a Greek god, I'd be Poseidon. He seems like a happier fellow than Zeus, and he doesn't have all the pressure."

In Boquete, where soft rains fell valley by valley, Amanda ran to every waterfall we came to on our hikes and beckoned us into the spray. We were already wet and muddy anyway, so come on! Our inn sat on a creek whose banks were speckled with brick-sized metamorphic rocks. Walker and Addison gathered them and began building a fort. Just eighteen inches high, it was more of a charmed circle: they stood inside it, arms around each other, best pals. On our last morning, when we discovered that someone had swept the rocks back into the river, I was much more upset than they were. A midlife mania for metaphor can make you construe innocuous reversals as catastrophic routs.

In 2004, I wrote a profile of Harold Ramis, the writer-director of *Caddyshack* and *Groundhog Day*. Though revered in the comedy world, Harold saw himself as "a benevolent hack." "Much as I want to be a protagonist, it doesn't happen, somehow," he told me. "I'm missing some tragic element or some charisma, or something. Weight. Investment."

He believed that his comedic partner, Bill Murray, had what he lacked. "One of my favorite Bill Murray stories is one about when he went to Bali," Harold said. "I'd spent three weeks there, mostly in the south, where the tourists are. But Bill rode a motorcycle into the interior until the sun went down and got totally lost. He goes into a village store, where they are very surprised to see an American tourist, and starts talking to them in English, going, 'Wow! Nice hat! Hey, gimme that hat!' " His eyes lit up. "Word gets around this hamlet that there's some crazy guy at the grocery, and he ended up doing a dumb show with the whole village sitting around laughing as he grabbed the women and tickled the kids. No worry about getting back to a hotel, no need for language, just his presence, and his charisma, and his courage. When you meet the hero, you sure know it."

I also spent some time with Stanley Donen, who directed

Charade and *Funny Face* and co-directed *On the Town* and *Singin' in the Rain.* When he talked about his place in the firmament, at age seventy-eight, he began to choke up. "Here it is," he was finally able to say. "As an artist, I aspire to be as remarkable as Leonardo da Vinci. To be fantastic, astonishing, one of a kind. I will never get there. He's the one who stopped time. I just did *Singin' in the Rain.* It's pretty good, yes. It's better than most, I know. But it still leaves you reaching up."

Day wrote three more novels before Mom got cancer. The first was a baggy saga about Indonesia, the second a choleric take on Swarthmore College, and the third, *The Deerlover,* a rambling examination of a suburban man named Cal who yearns for more. None found a publisher.

When Day asked me to read *The Deerlover,* I was still mad that he'd never said a word to me when Melanie and I broke up, a few months earlier. I also felt that his fiction was too seemly—that it lacked any wild rumpus. I didn't soften the blow much in my editorial note; the obligatory "There's a lot of good stuff here" sentence was just that, a sentence, even though he'd often told me, "A writer needs recognition of his achievement" and "Always compliment what's good, and recognize the effort involved." He gave and wanted to get the shit sandwich: "For there is always effort and achievement, even if, in the eyes of an expert, there is a flawed product; and it is life-denying not to acknowledge it."

When Day was in Warsaw, he told Mom he'd dreamed about the seven rejections *The Deerlover* had just received: "I awoke demoralized. Will I ever be a writer?" In his journals, he wrote, "I appear to myself as verbose, shallow, over-ambitious, vain; either unsophisticated or over-sophisticated. I have the feeling that my own writing has left me multiply wounded, devastated."

I loved the act of writing when I was deep in it, when every glance out the window registered fresh weather. The results were another matter. "Awkward and bloodless, not felt," I muttered, in my journals. And "My writing seems falsely cheerful, like an alcoholic with a facelift gibbering away with a cigarette waving." And "Gap between intent (a luminous evocation of success & failure in NYC) and execution (a few well-turned anecdotes)." And, most banefully, "Lacks New England snowfall!"

Flaubert observed that "Human speech is like a cracked kettle on which we beat out tunes for bears to dance to, when we long to move the stars to pity." The perfection of the sentence refutes its complaint. It's like Nabokov griping about how, as a native Russian, his prose in *Lolita* ("picnic, lightning") was necessarily "a second-rate brand of English." Oh, fuck you.

In her late sixties, Mom began writing again, secretly. After she died, I found a poem in her computer, "Steam Reassures Him." It later appeared in *The New Yorker*.

> *My husband is watching me iron.*
> *Steam reassures him. The hiss of starch*
> *The probing slide around each button of his shirt*
> *Speaks to him of Solway Street in Pittsburgh.*

As for me, the wicker basket is a reproach.
There is last summer's nightgown,
And several awkward round tablecloths
Which refuse to lie flat.

My house specializes in these challenges.
Bags of mail I did not ask to receive
Choke the floor of my linen closet.
A photograph of me, holding a baby on a beach.
But which beach and, for that matter, which baby?
A Japanese chest whose bottom drawer has irresponsibly
    locked itself,
And who can remember where I put the key?

That night, waiting for sleep, I whisper,
I did only trivial things today.
And he asks, Why aren't you painting?

I was Day's first reader, but he was not mine. I would find
my own way. Only when I wrote about Mom, in 2006, did
I ask him to read something before I published it. Aside
from his reservations about the role played by *The Tailor of
Gloucester*, his response was complimentary. His therapist
had warned him, "Do *not* enter into competition with Tad,
nor conform to his casting of your character."

A week after the piece appeared, we all went to Villanova for Christmas. A rash on Day's face had prevented him
from shaving for five weeks, so he looked unkempt, even
seedy. At our first dinner he gloomily announced that his
remaining life span had been "allotted by the actuaries at

the IRS as nine years." Then he asked to see the alternate photo layouts for the piece, photos of me and Mom when I was young. Examining them, he exclaimed, "How can you look at these photos and not know that your mother loved you?"

I was stunned. I knew that she loved me, and I was confident that the piece made that clear. I bit my tongue and held my temper, and Timmie defused the tension. But after dinner, I went into Day's bedroom, where he was tugging off his leather boots, to ask what that was all about. He said my portrait had been too harsh, after all. "It's *your* article and *your* career, and you will do with them what you like. You will do well—you have done well—and you will continue to do well. But this is my view," he said. "The emotional sterility is what troubles me."

"I feel extremely misunderstood," I said. He looked at me, levelly. "How can you say that about aridity, when your son is sitting across from you, obviously upset, and you're sitting there dry-eyed? *You're* the arid one, you've always been that way, and I wish you weren't. I so wish you weren't." He didn't say anything, so I went on. "I know you have feelings. But why, why do you have to present everything as a syllogism?"

He sighed and shot his cuff. "I have told others, and I don't know if I have told you, that you're my favorite living writer."

"You had mentioned that to me, and I appreciate it," I said, warily. I'd later find that he'd kept files of all of my articles.

But, he said, I'd become a prisoner of psychotherapy:

"Life is about saying yes to the mysteries of the future, not about endless refinements of the past."

"You're a historian!"

He opened his palms: "I'm a simple man who tries to live the questions of the moment."

"You're not at all simple," I said. "And do you really believe you're living this question with me, right now?"

He flushed. Then he shifted convulsively, as if he were molting, and said, "I suppose that in response to watching my father suffer so many defeats and humiliations, I overcompensated and became very well defended." After a moment, he added, "I appreciate your attacking me in such a sportsmanlike manner. And I do love you."

"And I love you, too," I said. He stood, wearing one boot, and we hugged. I just wished that I hadn't had to fight for it so.

When Amanda and I needed money, and I was trying to reinvent myself to make more, I began writing television scripts. A number of my friends were TV writers—Rich, my cross-country companion, was running *Family Guy*— and it seemed like something I could maybe do.

I wrote a drama pilot loosely inspired by Will Schenck's career at Condé Nast, and discovered that I loved creating a world. Then I wrote another, better pilot about a Wasp family that owns a failing gun company. The showrunners of *The Americans,* the FX series about Soviet spies in the United States, wanted to produce it, and suddenly I had a manager and a caramel-voiced agent.

But FX passed, and nobody else wanted it, either. FX

gave me a blind deal to write another pilot, and I began one about a separatist group creating its own country in Montana. Again, it had promise; again, the promise stalled. I wrote a screenplay with the actor-director Andrew McCarthy based on one of my *New Yorker* articles, a father-son story at sea. But he and I fell out, amicably enough, over how to tell the tale. We had each brought our own father to the script, which was at least one father too many.

I began developing a comedy with two musician friends about their life on the road. One of them pitched the idea to a well-connected pal of his, a comedian who'd had a show on HBO, and the comedian jumped aboard. It slowly became clear that my friend had neglected to tell the comedian that I was part of the project, too. He handled it with such clumsy ruthlessness that his future in Hollywood seems assured. I was hurt and I was mad, so it took me a few months to accept that he was probably right—it was a different show now, jokier and more improvisational, and I was no longer a great fit.

My agent gradually disappeared like the Cheshire Cat, leaving only a fulsome grin in midair. To get a project made you need a gripping story, talented collaborators, and luck, and I'd never been able to wrangle all three at once. For a while I continued to chase the caboose of the career I might have had, and then I stopped and watched it rattle into the distance.

In 2009, I published *Cheerful Money*. To limit the fallout, I asked Day to read it beforehand. He wrote to say that my portraits of his parents, Ted and Jess, were too cutting: "I feel that you write with a diamond stylus on crystal self-prepared, and believe that your reviews will say such in many positive ways. But gems are cold objects. May it not be possible to write, in future, in a way felt to be more loving and forgiving? That may actually ensure that the writing will be more enduring."

Steeling myself, I called him to suggest we talk through his concerns. He declined, saying, "Now you must do what you think best." I offered to send him the next draft for his further thoughts. "No, thank you."

I said, "Maybe you're not just concerned about Grandpa Ted and Grandma Jess, but about how *our* relationship comes across."

"That would be the standard Freudian couch vector," he replied. I didn't wave the receiver at my crotch, but I was tempted.

Several of Mom and Day's friends believed the book was too hard on them, and sent me notes of reproof. Ted Terry, after some kind words, added, "One key element, however, was missing: gratitude. You were blessed with two of the most loving, caring and supportive parents I have ever known. I hope that in time you will realize what an extraordinary gift you have received." Another Wasp wrote Day, "I thought that Tad is a very self-absorbed young man who extrapolated large themes from his own limited life experiences." (I was forty-seven.) Day replied that "what you say about parents and children is wise, and allows for any deficiencies of view on Tad's part, from which we pray he may emerge in due time of growth. Growing up includes, I think, forgiving parents for their insuperable deficiencies, as part of learning how limited oneself may be, and will inevitably be."

His note now seems to me both forbearing and wise. Yet he was stung by my portrayal. In his journal, he roughed out "On Reading a Family Memoir by my Firstborn Son":

a frosty, crusty one,
now that you may see yourself
as your eldest child sees you—
a distant, heavy pedagogue
from the ex-planet Pluto—
how shall you try to be,
how indeed?
a casual sort of asteroid,
unthreatening and small,
not predictable at all,
but willing to illuminate,
for its passersby in the universe,
one night's page of who they are:
that kind of
simple star

That same year, I gave a guest lecture to 150 students at Cal State Fullerton. In the Q and A, somebody asked which writers I admired, and I mentioned John Updike, and my sorrow that he'd died a few days earlier. There were nods of recognition, but only two or three.

In 2019, the thirty-seven-year-old poet Patricia Lockwood wrote a revisionist assessment of Updike in the *London Review of Books*. She was alive to the imagery of the early Ipswich novels: "Updike unrolls himself over the landscape of his boyhood like a vast horripilating skin. Hackles rise, pupils dilate, clean cold air crackles into the lungs. *Rabbit, Run* (1960), *The Centaur* (1963), and *Of the Farm* (1965) light up section by section, like a countryside freshly wired for electricity." But she went on to indict him for racism, anti-Semitism, homophobia, and misogyny— for the comprehensive constriction of an imagination that was never all that capacious: "He is like a God who spends four hours on the shading on Eve's upper lip, forgets to give her a clitoris, and then decides to rest on a Tuesday."

I felt sorry for Updike, because he was dead and defenseless and because she was right. Lockwood had anticipated this reaction, with its "strong flavor of people-are-being-mean-to-my-dad." In a brilliant judo move, she imagined Updike himself "sad in the clouds on my shoulder, baffled, as if he had especially been hoping that I would get it. I aimed it at you, he tells me: you were that vague spot a little to the east of Kansas." I also felt sorry for myself. The sense that a younger you would now see matters differently is the definition of growing old.

Lockwood liked Updike the appraiser best. She wrote that his criticism "is not just game and generous but able, as his fiction is not, to reach deeply into the objectives of other human beings, even to see into the minds of women. . . . He is pupilish and professorial all at once, and his valuations are often correct to the penny." That's the Updike I'd come to like best, too. Maybe because in his nonfiction he could just be Poseidon.

When Addison brooded about her friends—their fickleness, their indifference to deep feeling—or exploded about their shabby behavior, I told her that having a poet's sensibility is a blessing and a curse. Because she feels more, she'll be sad or angry more, especially in middle school, the Mariana Trench of human shittiness. But being able ringingly to express those feelings will be a great consolation. She absorbed this in silence, gazing past me toward her cloudy future self.

Provoked by *Cheerful Money*, Day began working on a memoir. He told me it would be a personal book, just for the family. Every few months he made a fresh start, only to repeat the same vignettes, the same strong early music. His father declaring that his mother had been "Laid, relaid, and parlayed by every man in Western Pennsylvania." "Stars Fell on Alabama" playing in the restaurant of his and Mom's honeymoon hotel. A four-man pissing contest, at the end of a college summer spent laying track on the Alaska Railroad, in which he came in last.

He returned most often to a night in a dance hall in the Philippine city of Zamboanga, when, as a twenty-seven-year-old bachelor, he got a crush on a "petite bright girl":

> *Whose eyes were luminous black pearl;*
> *More modest than the other girls*
> *With feathery downcast lashes.*
>
> *I promised I'd come back someday*
> *And left in an American way,*
> *Unceremoniously.*

Six months later, a bar girl in Manila told him, "She remember you, the one from Zamboanga. She want you to come and take her." He replied, guiltily, "I am very sorry.

But I cannot get back to Zamboanga." He was amazed that the dancer had been able to describe a nameless American so well that her message would eventually reach him in another bar five hundred miles away. Characteristically, he grappled with both the material perplexity—was there a bar-girl network he ought to have unearthed for his work?—and the immaterial one, the placenta of mystery that envelops a forgone opportunity. What would have happened if he'd gone back? Had that been his true fate? "I wonder if she ever thought of me after that," he wrote. "I certainly think of her, nearly sixty years later."

He didn't send me this material, but in 2017 he began mailing me poems, late offerings. "Reckonings on Reaching Age Eighty-Six" begins:

> *I am sorry about the novels I have not written—*
> *Fifteen of them perhaps—*
> *And sorry about the women I have not kissed—*
> *fewer than fifteen, using a standard of mutual attraction and*
> *accessibility.*
> *I am sorrier about the novels: only I could have brought*
>   *them to life*

A few weeks later, he sent "To My Dear and Derelict Father," which begins:

> *I do not see my face in yours—*
> *You were more handsome, and younger to the end.*
> *While I chose to a degree my own ugliness*
> *As a master of logics in history that only I could see.*

Therefore they did not mark my face
In a faint purple network
As alcohol did yours.

Also: your goodwill exceeded mine.
Your heart was more forgiving,
Having started with yourself.

I called Day to say that I liked being privy to his inmost thoughts. But he stopped mailing them.

I used to think that my job as a writer was to convey facts, description, a few bars of color, and a verdict. I gradually realized that how I responded to what I was writing about, how it made me feel, wasn't beside the point, but actually *was* the point. This discovery made me worry that I'd become a satrap of *The New Yorker*, which defaults to strenuous neutrality. Whenever I turned in a story and got an edited version back, the result—shorter, smarter, shorn of its wool—depressed me because it made manifest a nebulous, haunting truth: it was just another magazine piece, after all. I hadn't even threatened to escape my limitations.

I didn't leave, though, because it's a great magazine and because I felt that I was chipping away at a recurrent subject. Most of my best pieces were about people who, even at the summit of their success, felt that they'd failed. Triumph—rare, lucky, dull, and brief—is the engine of an airplane movie. It's an artifact of editing: failure, failure, failure, failure, a moment of triumph, and the story ends. If it continued, you'd see all the failure that followed. After the "Miracle on Ice" U.S. hockey team won the gold medal in 1980, only five of its twenty players had long careers in the NHL.

What unites us is aspiration that falls short. Fiction was still an appealing way to explore the subject, as it's unmatched in its capacity to portray interior life: consciousness, motivations, feelings. But if I couldn't read the minds of my own family, how could I inhabit those of made-up strangers? My real toads only remained real to me when I situated them in real gardens. Day turned to fiction so he could tell his story without having to wound anyone too much; I stuck with nonfiction to tell mine because I'd wound you if I had to. Sometimes I regard my slow-motion, oh-well choice of nonfiction as a capitulation, a failure. And sometimes I think that that feeling is only fitting.

After a day of reporting in Washington, DC, a long, muggy day made sultrier by all the lobbyists who'd hosed me with hot air, I visited Day on the way home. As usual, he was in the bathroom: banging-around sounds and "Fucks!" issued from the baby monitor. I ate a banana as an aide I hadn't met, a self-assured woman named Kanika, got Day into his pj's.

He sat on the edge of his bed, swallowing his seven pills one by one. "Do you want me to help you lay down now?" Kanika said—then corrected herself, "*Lie* down!" even as Day was saying, "It's 'lie,' not 'lay'!" She grinned at me, having heard this distinction before. He amuses strong women, which vexes him, which amuses them even more.

To forestall that dynamic, I said to him, "Do you remember how, when your brother, Charles, was in the hospital near the end, a nurse told him to just lay there quietly, and he corrected her the same way? And then said, 'I'm still the house grammatician'? And how, to make her feel better, you told her, 'That's okay—the word is 'grammarian'?'"

"I said that?" he said. I nodded, and he laughed. At the time, he'd told me that he'd hoped to talk with Charles about their childhood, but that it had seemed to be too late: "Charlie and I *never* talked about our parents. It was disturbed ground—too much wounding and bleeding."

Beginning to frown, he said, "I hope Charles didn't hear me."

"He didn't," I said. I had no idea—I wasn't there—but he seemed so concerned.

"That's good," he said. "*Grammarian.*"

"Was he your older brother?" Kanika said.

"Younger. Why do you ask?"

"You seem like you were a younger brother. Because you sometimes act like a big baby."

"And you sometimes act like a pain in the ass!"

She chuckled. "I was a middle child, that's probably why." Ignoring his scowl, she went on, "Now, let's get you lying down." They did, to muttered curses. When he was finally supine with the covers drawn up, she asked, "Would you like me to adjust the pillows?" and he bellowed, "No! Just leave me alone with my son."

Once Kanika had gone up to the kitchen, he said, "I can't stand her."

Knowing she could hear us on the monitor, I said, "She seems fond of you, actually."

A grin flitted across his face, but he shut his eyes, determined not to relinquish his grievance. So I said that I was finally writing another book.

"Good!" he said. His eyes popped open. "I think you have three memoirs in you, and you've only done one."

"What do you think this one should be about?"

"The alleged future," he said quietly, after a moment. I knew he was thinking that he probably wouldn't live to read it.

"And what should the last one be about?"

"Reflections and suppositions."

"So this one should look ahead and the last one should look back?"

"That's how it works." He shifted, settling. "Will this one be about squash?"

"There will be squash in it," I said. "But it can't all be about squash."

"Why the hell not?"

"That would reduce the readership even further."

"You're not trying to write a bestseller, are you?"

"I'm not trying to write a worst-seller, either."

He laughed, rumblingly, and winced. Then he sighed, a long, weary sigh, and pulled at his pillow, already forgetting.

"I should let you get some sleep," I said. "Do you need anything?"

"Only your company," he said. He reached out his hand. "Don't go just yet."

The ripples are reaching, have reached, their full amplitude. But the lake is glassy and you are still hugging the shore.

Tag

FROM THE air above Wainscott, as the red-tailed hawks see it and as I oversee it in dreams, the Georgica Association is a blaze of summer. Thirty-five shingle-style houses; softball games on the communal field with dogs running and kids circling the bases unhindered; four clay tennis courts presided over by an eighteenth-century windmill. The lone road splits, sheds a dead-end fork, then reunites to wing toward a gravel parking lot by the Atlantic.

Soaring east over the beach, you arrive at the bar between the ocean and Georgica Pond. Then north over the pond, skimming the shirred surface like a catboat, to touch down on our lawn. At the top of this landing strip, which wends past pitch pines and the birdbath where Amanda and I got married, stands Century House. Its three-riser steps beckon you to a porch that oversees our children racing across the grass in the wet late light.

Only on waking do you notice the mole runs, the thickets rife with ticks and poison ivy, and the stumps where hurricanes have thinned the pines to a last stand. The inroads.

Childhood is a boy curled like a comma, staring at his feet—those eccentric, Plutonian appendages. *Are they really mine?* Georgica is where my feet first tripped me up. They got wrinkled in the ocean, burned by the sun, stubbed when I slipped out of my flip-flops while biking, grassy from running on the lawn, and stayed sandy always, as I remembered, too late, every time I got into bed.

Century House, as the pencil marks on the bedroom doorframe attest, is where I grew up. The house of foxed books, the house with rain in its bones. We'd come out every August, often with Mom's brother, Paddy Pierson, and his family. Paddy, a *Wall Street Journal* reporter, was fizzy and funny, if sometimes twitchy with indignation; he and his wife, Karen, a photographer who could capture a late-afternoon mood, had three lively daughters a few years younger than us.

The house was owned by our great-uncle Wilson Pierson, who'd chaired the history department at Yale, and our great-aunt Letty, a painter and a preserver of beach-plum jam. Wilson—a Yale valedictorian like his brother, John, and their father, Charles—was formidable, and Letty's smile was hard to read. When her fourteen-year-old daughter Tisha, Norah's younger sister, didn't clean her room, Letty threw all of her clothes out the window. Yet when Mom was the same age and feared becoming a wallflower, Letty sent her yellow tulips from "A Secret Admirer."

Wilson and Letty mostly left us alone, aside from requiring us to be present and presentable for three meals a day (no bathing suits or bare feet); to clean our plates; to pick beans and zucchini from the garden; to fill the birdbaths and sweep the halls and plump the pillows and keep our voices down and stay clear during cocktail hour, which lasted two. Wilson's signature drinks, rattled up in a frosted shaker, included Mother-in-Law's Tongue, Ceiling Zero, and Autumn Haze (a lethal blend of curaçao, kirschwasser, almond liqueur, brandy, and vodka).

So it was here, benignly neglected, that I acquired many of the skills and habits and misapprehensions that constitute a rudimentary adult. Or at least a rudimentary adult in that Caucasian Chalk Circle. Here is where I learned to play tennis; to bodysurf; to admire moon snail shells and horseshoe crab stingers; to fly a kite and glory in fireworks; to play Parcheesi, Chinese checkers, hearts, and bridge; to read James Bond novels; to talk to people at parties; to dance; to drive; to drink beer; to drink wine; to drink Scotch; and to try sex on the beach—both the vodka-and-peach-schnapps cocktail and the sandy midnight experience.

The other houses of my childhood are gone, discarded shells. This is the inviolate one. But it's been under the gun since the seventies, when Wilson and Letty sold nearly half their land, the back two acres, to buy more time. Last summer, I bent to retrieve a tennis ball stuck under the chicken wire behind the courts. As I oodged my racquet to roll the ball out, I had a flashback to probing under that very stretch of wire when I was eight or nine. Ball in hand, I turned back, uneasily. Time had tossed its heavy mantle over me for a moment, the way we tossed towels over the kids when they were small. *Peekaboo!*

*   *   *

A month after Walker and Addison were born, we came out here for a week. On the last morning, we finally made it to the beach, carrying the kids in BabyBjörns. As Amanda adjusted Addison's bonnet, I said, "We should put salt water on their lips, so it will seep into their memories and they'll want to come back forever and ever."

Grand Day held Walker on his lap and they stared at each other. "Searching for meaning the way your father used to do," Day said.

"Before I gave it up," I said.

He laughed. "Did I ever tell you what Grandma Tim said?" His voice was soft. "She took you in her arms out on the lawn at Maplewood when you were less than a year old, and she came back dazzled by the way you took in everything with your eyes."

That week meant so much to us and so little to Addison and Walker—a ratio that would reverse, year by year.

In 2015, Day hosted a "Century Party." We invited everyone we knew within ten miles for cocktails on the lawn—repayment for the parties always popping off around us, steel drums in the distance. No remarks were planned, but Day stood on the corner of the porch and rapped on a champagne glass. He was eighty-four, but he'd just been jumping, gently, on the trampoline out back, and when we all did planks on the lawn he'd held his for more than a minute. Steady pitcher in Sunday softball, doughty walker by the dunes, he'd become a local institution.

He explained that the house had been built in the late nineteenth century by a Yale professor, William Dwight Whitney, with money he'd made from editing the ency-

clopedic *Century Dictionary*. "We decided to have a double
century celebration, because my late wife Elizabeth's grandfather, Charles Pierson, bought this house one hundred years
ago, in 1915. It's still called Century House by those who
care, though it doesn't say that on the sign out front. But
you're the intimates, the high intimates, who know this fact."

Gazing around at the upturned faces, he said he'd first
come here in 1959, but "my brother-in-law, John Pierson, has
been here longer than me." Paddy, wearing a pink sport coat,
waved from a nearby perch, the same agitatedly comical wave
his mother used to make when she'd cry "Leave it lay where
Jesus flang it!" Paddy and his family owned the house with
Day and us. After Norah died, in 2007, the Piersons wanted
to sell it, but we didn't. We had to rent the place out for most
of the summer to pay the upkeep, and it lacked the amenities
most renters demand—a pool, central air, a reliable stove—so
we wanted to modernize, but they didn't. There was further
strife about who got which weeks in August.

Day concluded, whimsically, "You know the principals
now, and if you have any questions, catch me privately!"

As the slabs of his personality shifted, in a late tecton-
ics, you could glimpse the boy he might have become if
he'd ever been encouraged. He'd declare, "There is no such
thing as allergies! There are only colds and sneezes!"—then
snicker at hearing such poppycock. One night at dinner, he
claimed that he'd spent the day kayaking around the pond
and baking cupcakes, two activities he'd have hated even in
his prime. Chortling, he favored us with a rare open grin.

In 2010, he recorded that he'd transfixed a wide range
of people at two Georgica parties: lesbians, gays, teenagers,
older women. "I think my eye patch had a lot to do with it,"

he wrote—he'd just had surgery for a detached retina—but he added, "I enjoy banter or serious discourse on any lines at all, as long as comedy may be in play and tragedy held at bay. *Talk* with me. I will *hear* you."

For a time, anyway. After one barbecue, Mary chastised him for getting sloshed. "I certainly don't want to embarrass my children, or Mary, or to degrade myself in the eyes of others," he wrote, vowing to "open up" at parties with bottled water. Maybe he forgot.

After Mom died, we didn't take many family photos, but every summer we'd assemble for one here for Day's Christmas card: kids and grandkids in the doorway of the windmill or on our lawn, the whole smiling clan.

We rarely leave the house at night, preferring dinners at the long mahogany table, where clam and whelk shells painted with your name indicate your place. Georgica is where the in-laws shine. Sara's humor lands in gleaming darts, and she does laundry faster than we can generate it, sneaking in, even after we've insisted that she stop, to produce another ziggurat of neatly folded towels. And Scott sparkles with a virtuosic display of sounds—bird whistles, a steaming teapot—and with his epic tale, begged for nightly by our five children, the cousins, about a wandering oil tanker called Happy Little Suez Max.

It's not easy fetching up late as an in-law in Georgica. In Day's fourth summer here, in the early sixties, he found his path to the beach barred by a local matriarch: "Who are *you?*" After that, as he couldn't swim anyway, he never went to the beach much. He sunned himself in a lounge chair on the lawn, organized rackety Saturday soccer games on the field, and scheduled late-afternoon walks with friends, timed so he could still calibrate the world's imperfections over cocktails with Wilson. He once walked so far he came back tottering and pale; Letty eyed Day as if he were a horse with strangles and said, "Throw a blanket over him."

Smitten by the place, Day took periodic notes toward a novel. In 1991 he wrote, "A few nights after the hurricane passed, a full moon rose pink over Trippe's old mansion at the end of the dunes and glinted opalescent into the water. Sky and water deepest of blue, moon and mirrored moon palest pure pink, until (half a drink, a conversation later) all was yellow and ordinary."

Late twilight is my favorite hour here, too. The crickets tune up with the Canada geese, that thrilling symphony, and the homes across the pond are flecked with light. Bicycling home on the dimming road, tires crunching the gravel, I pass the secret passage through the Samponaros'— the way I used to take as a shortcut home. The Samponaros left decades back and the path is overgrown with swamp mallow, but you can still make out how it was, and half-believe that if you could knife through the brambles as the rabbits do you'd emerge at the far end as a boy.

For decades, our neighbor George Willis preserved our sense of the place. He would drop to one knee to take group photographs, bald head bent over the viewfinder, then remember to send everyone copies. He played two sets of tennis one morning—he had masterly strokes but velveted them to keep the game fun for all—and sailed his ketch around the pond that afternoon. After pulling the boat up and covering it with a tarp, he collapsed against it: a mas-

sive coronary. "George had a beautiful death," Uncle Wilson said, pulling his nose so his voice wouldn't break.

Every Monday night there's an association-wide beach picnic that Mom always found stressful. Amanda, likewise. All
those separate blankets, island nations with inscrutable protocols. I enjoyed the picnics, though, the milling about with
a beer in hand. I'd loved parties since a high school baccha-
nal in Rob Nikpour's attic where I made out with one girl,
then another—toppling in a cloud of Genesee Cream Ale
and Baby Soft perfume—then backed our station wagon
through the Nikpours' hedge while driving off with a third.
And everyone made it home alive!

Amanda was drawn to Georgica at first. But when we
were struggling she began to resent its expensively preserved ease. And didn't my loyalty to Century House's bat-
tered side tables indicate that I, too, was stuck in time?

After Uncle Wilson died, in 1993 (unbeautifully, of prostate cancer), Norah began renting the place for most of the
summer to keep it solvent. The time her parents bought
had run out. She placed a granite stone engraved with
REMEMBER at the base of the tall red cedar; her grandfather
had planted the tree after he bought the property, and John
and Wilson used to jump over the sapling as boys. Her other
updates were less immemorial. Mended wicker chairs and
fountain-penned signs that warned against flushing anything of substance gave way to quick-fix fixtures from
Kmart, ceramic hands fluting in weird welcome, and the
pipes in the kitchen being painted a trippy blue and affixed

with a trail of plastic ants. She was holding on for us with a grip both New Age and arthritic.

When Walker was four, he'd play "Family" with Timmie and Scott's daughter, Lucia. They'd lie on the porch cushions, pretending to be asleep, then wake and stretch elaborately before saying, "Let's go check on the children!" Down the porch steps they'd tumble to pull a dish towel off "the children"—Pier and Sara's dog, Hershey. As Hershey jumped and spun, Walker and Lucia would throw their arms high in celebration. How happy this made me. Or when Addison shouted, "Daddy, Daddy!" as she ran through the house to find me: "There was a whale at the beach!" Watching them awaken, amazed by the world.

The cousins' favorite evening pastime is flashlight tag. Two or three hunters use flashlights to seek the hiders, local kids from the tennis program and those parents willing to be cajoled, who flit between shrubs or go to ground behind the cottage. Once caught you sit on the porch with the other captives and eye the tennis-ball can on the lawn, hoping someone will streak from the dark to kick it over and set everyone free.

The game is insanely exciting: stabs of light approaching as you slink from fir to fir or fling yourself into a chokeberry bush, trying not to breathe. Amanda, who wears a black ninja outfit to compete, has gotten heart palpitations from the adrenaline. Addison, wary of low branches that grabbed at her cat's-ears headband, liked to hide with an adult to steady her nerves, but Walker, who started talking up that evening's game at breakfast, was masterly at apparating to kick the can. On Labor Day, he'd forlornly bid his best hideouts farewell.

*   *   *

The gallery of photos in the front hall evokes the history of the place in its people, merriment, like memory, diminishing as the years roll back. A grinning portrait of Norah sits beside one of her parents, Wilson and Letty, beaming on their wedding day, forty years earlier—Letty in a Sonja Henie dress; Wilson in spats, with a sprig of baby's breath in his lapel. Beneath them is a picture of Charles Pierson, a gimlet-eyed eminence, with his wife, Elizabeth, radiant in Gibson Girl white. Hearing of "Goggy Pierson" only as a doddery painter of bland seascapes, I could not imagine this incandescent youth.

The central image, to me, is a photo Karen Pierson took on the porch in 1972, using a timer: Wilson, slightly self-conscious about wearing an apron he'd put on to do the dishes, and Letty, staring down the camera as if it were an approaching storm, are surrounded by Mom and Day and Paddy and Karen and the six of us cousins, all packed in and smiling. Above these portraits, this baton pass of the generations, is a verse from Isak Dinesen:

> *Let the old ones be remembered now;*
> *They once were gay and free.*
> *And that they knew to love, my dear,*
> *The proof thereof are we!*

Norah appointed Pier the next property manager; he has the kind of sturdy back on which the world heaps burdens. Paddy was mad that Norah hadn't chosen him, the obvious heir from her generation, but I was delighted that she hadn't chosen me, as the job required patience and diplomacy. Pier maintained his responsible, Day-like exterior, but immediately began worrying about hurricanes and fires and moles and finding new renters and tackling the vast menu of deferred maintenance, just as Mom would have done. Claw-footed tubs sized for seals were replaced with generous tubs or shower stalls; the laundry room, with its lathed plywood, was completely rebuilt; the knob-and-tube wiring came out, room by room; fresh cedar shingles clad each side of the house in turn.

The rift with the Piersons widened with every project. Paddy would hug you fiercely on arrival and then stand back, his jaw working; he'd developed neurological issues, and soon could no longer speak, so Karen now voiced the Piersons' views on the house. It began to feel like the Siege of Ostend, an exhausting clash both sides would lose. It began to feel like we'd have to sell.

Us, the Piersons, and Uncle Wilson and Aunt Letty
on the porch in Wainscott.

After the Century Party it got harder, every summer, to manage Day. We'd hide the rum bottle and stay close to keep him from falling on the hard fir floors. When he crept down the staircase from his bedroom, I'd descend backward before him, hands spread like a guard playing D. He'd grip the railing with his right hand, place the cane on the next step down with his left, then negotiate the riser with a questing left foot. After a grunt or an oath, he'd hurl his right foot down and crash into me, so I had to dig my heels in to keep us both upright. His feet were no longer cooperative—he'd sit on his bed and stare at them, those swollen satellites—so the sixteen steps took three minutes. It was like running after Walker and Addison when they were toddlers, only backward and in slow motion.

He often began his descent without ringing the bell we'd given him to summon help, and I foresaw him breaking a hip on the stairs. I also foresaw myself, at his age, reveling in these mutinous forays. He was so plainly delighted when he stumped into the kitchen one morning, on his own, to ask, "Any yogurt?"

For years, the front hall table would accrue banged-up trophies from Georgica's tennis tournaments. Pier, who has a crushing serve and forehand, usually won the men's singles; Sara, rock solid, often won the women's; and they'd team to win the mixed doubles. Only in 2018, when Sara's gimpy leg kept her off-court, did the latter trophies go elsewhere. Pier and I were also a good bet in the men's doubles, which we won fifteen times. I lost the power on my serve during the Clinton administration, but we rampaged at net. Doubles lets you cloak some frailties.

In 2019, the table stayed bare. Pier and I were a step

slow, a beat off sync. And Sara's leg problem, devastatingly, had turned out to be ALS.

In the summer of 2018, we got so worried about Day falling in Wainscott that we prevailed on Dr. Bowles to tell him he couldn't come. He still acquiesced to doctors, except when they told him to use his walker or wear his compression stockings or do his occupational therapy exercises or eat less salt and sugar and syrup and ice cream. Dr. Bowles told me, "The important thing is to let him be angry and let him control as much as he can." Day was furious. So we let him control his rage by channeling it toward her: "It'd be great if you came, but *Dr. Bowles* says . . ." The way you say, "It's up to Santa."

While we were in Wainscott, Janice Duffin called to report that Day had reached a new stage. He hadn't mounted the four steps to the kitchen in five days. He needed a lift chair to sit up and a wheelchair to go to the bathroom, and he was on allopurinol for gout, gabapentin for restless leg syndrome and neuropathy, senna and Miralax for constipation, mirtazapine and liquid Prozac for depression, and oxycodone for generalized pain. Janice told me, "He seemed very sad yesterday, so I said, 'This getting old isn't easy, is it?' And he said, 'This isn't getting old.'"

When we were young, Day, busy at Swarthmore, would come out for just a week. Now Amanda, busy at Food52, came out for just a week. The company was growing and had been celebrated in *Inc.* and *Fast Company*. First we could pay our taxes on time, then we could repay our parents' loans, then we could start saving for retirement, and then President Obama appointed Amanda to the commission that selected

White House Fellows. She began to see herself not just as a survivor, but as a success, and gratitude sluiced back into our lives. But constraint had become our new normal, like a drop ceiling, installed to lower heating costs during the energy crisis, that you forget to remove later.

At the end of the week, we'd pick Amanda up at the jitney stop, the kids hiding in the no-streetlight dark to jump out. Flashlight tag folded us all back into the mix. Sixty seconds to scatter; go! When I wasn't tearing around with Addison, I used the hidey-holes from my childhood. As I crouched under a fir near Mary Petrie's fence, a wedge of geese scudded overhead and their wingbeats, a vast shuddering circumflex accenting all of us below, carried me back to 1972. Mom was just about to step onto the porch and call "Yoo-hoo! Bedtime!"

Half of her ashes are in Bryn Mawr, but half are here, buried under the hydrangea bush and scattered in the pond. She is only mostly gone.

We made the Piersons an offer to buy their share of the house, a kind of Hail Mary. When we'd gathered to discuss what to do, Day's face was a study. He wanted the Piersons out, but he hated dipping into capital. Finally, laying his head on the table exhaustedly, he murmured that he'd kick in a sizable sum. "That's very generous," Pier said. "But I think we're going to need a larger cash call." Day eventually raised his opening bid significantly, even though we'd since told him that he couldn't come to the house anymore— a big chunk of his assets going to underwrite Mom's twelfth major project, the one she hadn't foreseen.

Needing money for Paddy's care, among other reasons,

the Piersons began to negotiate. Paddy died that winter, but the talks continued for three more months. I was handling the discussions with their representative, an investment banker they knew who was formidably civil, subtle, and resolute. There were numerous issues to settle, including how many years they'd continue to share in the proceeds if we sold the place, and how that share would step down over time. To get anywhere with the banker I had to keep threatening to walk, which was easier after he suavely reneged on agreed-upon points, but which I found debilitating.

One night, Amanda said that I was going about it wrong—that I'd been too empathetic, given too much away.

"It's not simply a transaction where you try to win," I said, dejectedly. "It's also going to determine how we all feel about each other afterward."

The next day, she came to me and said, "I know you're doing your absolute best, and I'm sorry for what I said." Her startling apology felt as big as the sale itself. Maybe we were still capable of change.

The first medical bulletins from Janice filled me with dread. But I found it somewhat consoling to confirm what-ever plan she suggested, and to know that she could at least ensure that Day wasn't drinking. His health was another staircase he was descending: a lunge downward, then a gathering before the next fall. As Day himself didn't seem concerned, I began to take his descent almost in stride.

When I FaceTimed with him after the transaction with the Piersons closed, he was lying in his new hospital bed, alongside the four-poster, slurping cranberry juice through a straw. *Sprawk!*

"Thank you for what you did today," I said. "I hope it will keep the house in the family for years to come."

"What did I do?" he asked, testily. I reminded him about the sale of the house. "This house?"

"No, the house in Wainscott. Where all of us go every summer." *Almost all.*

"Did we buy or sell?"

"We bought."

He leaned back, as if basking on his lounge chair. "Good," he said. "I'm very glad."

We cleaned out the attic and the garage and jettisoned four trucks' worth of ancient material, from brittle wicker furniture to molted garden hoses to grumbly old freezers to Norah's ceramic hands to steamer trunks that collapsed when you opened them to cigar boxes labeled "Old Miscell" to a raft of Goggy Pierson still lifes that we finally, seventy years on, had the courage to commit to the deep. In September, the Piersons drove out to retrieve some chairs and cookware from Norah's cottage. Karen collected a photo of Paddy, young and resolute, from the photo wall, as well as one of her daughters with Wilson and Letty's Norwich terriers. "Oh, dear, I can't believe it's the last time!" she cried, her eyes sweeping the reproachful rooms in dismay.

Over the winter, we would undertake most of the renovations we'd been eyeing for years, a fireworks finale. Each of our three families had enough put aside to split the assessment; we'd become savers, like Day—with an impulse to spend it all down, like Mom. Amanda and Timmie managed the project, which entailed an enormous amount of discussion of tiles and dimmers and door pulls, an even more enormous amount of yelling at our upcharging contractor, and saving gales of laughter.

We gutted Norah's cottage to build in a loft and a working kitchen, with a ramp for Sara. We replaced the flashing on the west wall of the main house and installed central air. We redid the kids' bathroom on the third floor, installing two sinks and a rainhead shower so they'd no longer descend on our bathrooms every evening at 6:00 P.M., leaving a trail of sandy footprints.

The biggest change was knocking down walls to establish an open kitchen and dining room; now you can see the ocean from the stove. Timmie and Amanda wanted to transform a cramped cell where we grumpily took turns cooking into a festive gathering place, complete with a breakfast nook where you can read the paper and chat with passersby. To get each new shelf sized exactly, Amanda measured pots and pans and boxes of Saran Wrap, just as Mom did in Villanova with loaves of bread. These devotions made her feel, or understand, that the house was hers, too, at last.

I kept expecting a shirty email from some family elder decrying this pernicious embrace of light and air. But it was just us now.

On the last weekend, Walker played in the boys' singles final. At thirteen, he'd begun to hit with topspin and had developed a reliable serve to complement his ground strokes, but his opponent had more power. As the points extended to twenty and thirty shots, it became an attritional war. Walker's tongue poked out and a rim of sweat shone on his upper lip; he worked like a sapper defusing a bomb. It was exhausting to suppress my body English as his droopier efforts plooped toward the net. He eventually took it, 6–4, 6–3. "It was such a boring match," he said, nonchalantly toting the trophy home.

The final game of flashlight tag was epic but cool; the weather invariably shifts on Labor Day weekend, as if the place were taking leave of us. Afterward, I put the kids to bed under the eaves. Walker muttered some indistinct praise of Hershey—he and Addison both still desperately wanted a dog—and conked out. As I tucked the russet blanket from my boyhood over Addison, she resumed her periodic line of metaphysical inquiry, her form of the aerial view: "What happens after we die, Daddy?"

"I don't know. Some people, like Lorna"—their beloved first babysitter—"believe we go to heaven."

"That would be so nice," she said. "To see everyone you loved again."

"Yes, it's a very appealing idea," I said. "I'd love to see Foffie again, and to know that eventually I'd see you guys." I maybe should have left it there. "Unfortunately, I don't see any evidence that heaven exists." Addison frowned. "Maybe this life is it, in which case the whole point is to make the most of it."

"Or reincarnation," she said, after a moment. "I'd love to come back in another universe, but with a memory of this life."

"But if that happened—which would be very cool!— why don't we recall our earlier lives in other universes?"

She worked the problem, tucking her stuffed dog, Kai, under her chin. "Maybe this is the very first one," she said. Her breathing slowed until it matched the waves breaking across the bar. "Or maybe this is heaven."

Hand-Me-Downs

A BLUE heron emptied Day's pond of koi, one of the house's downspouts fell into the hedge, and both deck doors sagged on their hinges. We fixed all that, but after his bathroom sink dripped on through three repairs we closed the valve. Even Day's plumber had grown fatalistic.

Whatever wasn't collapsing was essentially in open storage, the house a neglected museum. Most of the exhibits were Mom's, and easy to gloss. Closets packed with empty Bonwit Teller boxes (just the thing for Christmas gifts); drawers cram-full of threadbare blue and red towels (once royally plush); packing boxes stuffed with her great-grandmother's china and champagne glasses (unopened since the move to Swarthmore in 1973); paintings and unfinished canvases piled in her third-floor studio, where a hot plate with coffee cups and a jar of Sanka from circa 1994 resembled a deadpan installation piece (caffeinated coffee kept her awake for two days, just as a mai tai knocked her flat).

Then there were Day's books, more than 2,500 of them. Too few and various for a university's Southeast Asia collection; far too numerous for the local library sale. I asked him how he wanted to handle all these belongings. "That will be an issue for my heritors," he said grandly, as if janissaries from afar would arrive to oversee the dispersal rather than it falling to, say, me.

When Amanda and I were window-shopping in Bangkok on our delayed honeymoon, I drew her eye to a crown prince Buddha. Carved in northern Burma nearly three hundred years earlier from a single piece of teak, it had been lacquered the color of chocolate ice cream, then scuffed and scarred by the centuries. Yet beneath his jagged crown the Buddha's smile felt timeless. His mudra—left hand sideways palm up, meditating; right dipping to touch the earth—symbolized the moment of enlightenment, when his rage became wisdom.

We circled the block a few times, weighing the budget-wrecking cost: nearly five thousand dollars. Amanda observed that I'd come into our marriage with Cambodian Buddha heads, a Thai monk statue, and an Indian Trimurti, and that we'd just picked up a stone sadhu in Kochi. She worried that our book-laden apartment was beginning to resemble a historian's study—a certain historian's study— and was determined that we maintain our developing "Let's try it and see" design scheme. I pointed out that we had a wall that displayed the rap sheets of minor criminals from rural Georgia, and that an oversized pink-and-green knockoff Knole sofa bulked in our living room like an El Camino. "True . . ." she said, searching my face. "Okay!"

Her hopefulness killed me then because I wanted to live up to it. It killed me later because I hadn't.

As a boy, I admired Day's striped nylon watch straps. He paired these zips of color with Lacoste polos for a sporty look that J.Crew and I would build our summer collections around. In high school, when I was a lanky sprig, I'd dart into his closet and slip one of his Lacostes into my book bag before heading to school, where I'd layer it over my button-down shirt, aiming at preppy and landing on scraggy.

In 1989, I picked up a Rolex in Singapore that kept day-date time and had a slinky stainless-steel band and that classic heft, but featured chic red numerals. That's because it was a fake. It was an artful fake, though, like 1989 me. Day admired it, and when he and Mom passed through Singapore a few years later, she asked me where she could get him one. Day's desire for a counterfeit Rolex puzzled me at the time, but in his journal he described himself as "a watch-conscious man who never buys a timepiece, but relies on the cheap old Omega on his wrist." I told Mom where to find the shop, Lee's, what to ask for, and how to bargain. She took a taxi over—but Lee's had been shut by the police. She approached some nearby peddlers, fully expecting to be arrested, and hastily chose the world's worst fake Rolex. Weightless as a balloon, it broke within six months.

Day usually preferred heirlooms that were conspicuously immemorial. He preserved two of his grandfather's grandfather clocks as well as his mantel clock, and in 2012, tidying up his safe-deposit box, he sent me the gold Patek Philippe pocket watch that belonged to that grandfather, Theodore Wood Friend, Sr. "I am happy that you are the fourth Theodore in our line," he wrote, "a happiness augmented by our decision to give you a different middle name, so that you would not be 'IV.'" The watch felt pleasing in my palm, but it carried no mojo for me, no thrilling Theodorehood. I never liked the name—as a child, I'd write it with the "d" reversed: "Theobore."

Three years later, Day wrote us from Pittsburgh in a melancholy mood after attending a memorial service for an old friend.

All this is occasioned by memory of Henry Hoffstot, who went for 75 years to his law office at Reed, Smith, until the month of his death at age 97. And who left for me in a little envelope (how he came by it, I do not know) a rather tiny wristwatch (early in its 20th century popularity), inscribed on the back of its silver casing to "T.W. Friend Jr / February 28th, 1915." That was my father's twelfth birthday. The gold minute hand is missing.

By then, he felt the burden of these mortmains: a hundred-year-old gift, from a family that gave gifts in lieu of love, now given to him. At best, an empty vessel for ancestral memories; at worst, a busted trifle. What do you do with that? He had it cleaned and gave it to Amanda for Valentine's Day.

Late one summer night when I was twenty-three and shifting apartments, I moved all my worldly belongings in a taxi. But possessions accrue, and begin to possess you. My tuxedo, with its tin-pot-dictator shoulders, is pure late-

eighties camp, but I associate it with those black-tie parties at *Spy*. My Order of Lenin medal, a gold-and-platinum
relic I picked up in Prague in 1991, has never drawn anyone's notice, but it reminds me of my backpacking days and
the fall of the Berlin Wall. And I'm inordinately fond of the
tambour desk I bought from Uncle Wilson's estate, whose
brass fittings feature blooming flowers, honeycombs buzzing with bees, and an inscription suited to Pierson valedic-
torians: NOTHING WITHOUT LABOR.

I must tell Addison and Walker not to take that admo-
nition too seriously, that it's an inside joke. Because the
weightiest hand-me-downs are habits of mind. I've come
to see myself as a mint-fudge brownie baked from an old
family recipe: on top, a layer of Day—the rectangular
head, long ears, and stiff-necked physicality. Then a green
stripe of Mom's dinner-party persona: playful and tenacious. And at bottom the fudgy substrate of Day's inex-
tirpable solitude—the part I cannot hand back and must
not hand on.

When the kids were in eighth grade, we went skiing in
Colorado. In the hotel's convenience store, I noticed that
Walker was drawn to a skinny plush-toy bird covered with
rainbow-colored hair, a kind of drip-painted Lorax. It was
spectacularly ugly and crazed-looking. The morning of our
departure, Walker carried it to the counter as I was buying
coffee and granola bars for the trip and mutely positioned
its face next to his. Two pairs of beseeching eyes.

"Do you really *need* that?" I said. "Couldn't you borrow
a lovey from Addison's vast zoo?"

He put the bird back, impassively. Behind him, Addison

widened her eyes and mouthed, "He loves it!" So I bought it and slipped it over his shoulder to peck him on the cheek, and he buried his face in its scratchy hair.

We didn't have a dog, but we did have Psycho Dodo.

We hired a conscientious woman named Elizabeth Stahl to begin a cull of Day's house. She would sort, toss, and box. She and I started upstairs, where he hadn't been since about 2012, and angled toward the heart of the house. I introduced Elizabeth to Day one morning, having vaguely explained her role to him, and they shook hands. He didn't really take her in, because he could no longer lift his head to establish his trademark eye contact. "Just so long as she doesn't get in my way," he said later, which was funny if you thought about it just the right amount.

I showed her the valuables: the silver; the Georges Rouault lithograph; the graceful, whiskey-colored dressers and desks. And I made note of a few small things I cherished: a photo of Grandma Jess, age four, cuddling a black kitten just after her beloved father died of peritonitis. A handmade fireplace broom, once Grandma Tim's. And a white bowl speckled with blue dots in which Mom made chocolate mousse for my birthday.

As we took inventory, I realized I had no idea which objects meant the most to Day, because no one talked about that sort of thing much aside from Mom and Marcel Proust. The framed photo of him with George H. W. Bush in China? The wedding photos of him and Mom, shyly glowing? The frescoes of me and Pier and Timmie when we were small? The Lord Bima shadow puppet I got for him in Indonesia? Knowing which possessions he treasured wouldn't make me preserve them, necessarily; the past is already adhesive enough. It might help me understand him better, though.

I miss the radio of my youth: the gravelly DJs on WMGK and WMMR, the serendipitous playlists, the drug-like jolt of golden songs. The purest hit for me, still, is "Night Moves," by Bob Seger & the Silver Bullet Band. It came out in late 1976, but I only noticed it in 1978, after I got my driver's license and began tooling down Route 320, which led both to school and to an AMC movie theater where I had a number of B– dates.

Seger's muted opening G chord transformed that mall-dense landscape, lacquering it with hormonal promise.

Out past the cornfields where the woods got heavy
Out in the back seat of my '60 Chevy
Workin' on mysteries without any clues
Workin' on our night moves

His sandy voice fit his hypnotic strumming: down, down-up-down, down-up-down, down-up, up, up, and away to a pulsating E minor promise that I'd find my own black-haired beauty with big dark eyes. "Night Moves" was about sex, of course—Topic A in the pop curriculum. But it felt much larger. It felt like ache stripped of adolescent self-pity, ache unadulterated. The song made me realize that deep feeling could be more than a bewildering series of ephemeral torments. That you could shuck it outward into art.

I didn't really get that Seger was exploring the gap

between feeling and understanding, summer and winter, youth and age; that's only clear now. "Started hummin' a song from 1962," he rumbles, recalling the distant thunder of his teenage years—and it all floods back. "Oh!" he cries, and "Ooh!" and "I remember!" and "Yeah, yeah, yeah!" over and over, a crescendo that reenacts the encounters in his '60 Chevy.

I could play "Night Moves" for Walker and Addison, but it feels impossible to explain all that—and probably unwelcome, anyway. The Museum of Your Father's Youth draws very few tourists.

At thirteen, Walker began sleeping twelve hours a night, going as far away as I went in my naps and returning equally poleaxed. He and Addison had their own rooms now, and she often closed the door to hers. We were racing toward that moment in their trajectory when our role, as booster rockets, is to fall burning back to earth.

But not quite yet. At night, Walker runs into our room and dives onto the bed between us to help us with the *Times*'s "Spelling Bee" ("Nanny?"; "Tyrant?") so we can become a collective Genius. Addison, a more meticulous flosser, arrives a few minutes later and burrows alongside. When I note that it's way past bedtime, she skillfully changes the subject by asking Amanda about the Instagram Live she just did. "Mommy, you're a warrior, so beautiful and strong!" she says, tunneling deeper.

Snuggling between us, Walker likes trying to breathe in tandem with me or Amanda, but he's always surprised by how slow our metabolisms are. Gasping sleepily, he puts his arms around me and conks his head against mine: "See you in the

early times!" He's readopted the phrase, probably because I
kept recalling it so fondly. The other night, on his way to bed,
he placed the Mongolian crown he wore to play "Invisible"
atop the crown prince Buddha, certifying it at last.

Walker's invocation of the early times reminded me that I
had all those Handycam tapes . . . somewhere. I eventually
found the camera behind the sofa in my study, charged it
up, and started watching.

I had forgotten the kids' smeared bibs and jammy faces,
the matey way they'd paw each other's noses. I had forgotten how Addie clenched her fists around her bottle and
cleaned the tabletop with a piece of bread, and her habit of
turtling her neck and pursing her lips, like a lord in Parlia-
ment rising to dispute, then motorboating her food all over
us. I had forgotten Walker's ability to sob once and then
tremble his lower lip, the picture of adorable misery, or
how he would go boneless to forestall being put down for
a nap. I had forgotten all the runny noses and Motrin doses
and nights of "Goodnight nobody." I had forgotten the
phase when they industriously depillowed the couch and
the phase when they pushed our chairs from room to room
and the phase when they ran counterclockwise around the
dining table, roaring. I had forgotten "Tow Truck": they'd
get on my back when I was on all fours and I'd rumble
around for a while, spinning and snorting, then dive into
an underground garage as they tumbled off. I remembered
that we called them "The Squeakers," but I had forgotten
that it was because they made so many little noises, so many
purrs and cries, that the squeaking was constant.

I had forgotten Deb and Paul cackling together in our

kitchen (its cherrywood cabinets now painted a creamy white; they, long divorced). And a dozen friends unsnapping their Björns and dropping their babies into our Friday night music group, where over beer and pizza we'd sing "The Wheels on the Bus" and "Baby Beluga" (we've lost touch with half of them). And Amanda's grandmother Helen making Thanksgiving dinner in her nineties, good-humored but stone-deaf, laughing at a joke no one had made. After a harrowing final year, she died at 102.

When the kids were eleven months old, I had filmed Addie as she led Walker on a crawl out of the kitchen. She wore a pink top and red bloomers, he a onesie and a bib. Their hands slapped the wooden floor stickily. Walker looked back, a tiny Orpheus: was I still following? He turned and padded back to sit below me, gazing up with searchlight eyes.

Addie pulled herself up on the gate we'd installed between the hall and the living room beyond, which was washed with morning light. Unable to open the door in the gate—there was a thumb release up top—she shook the bars furiously. Walker joined Addie and tried to stand alongside her. But he couldn't, quite. He looked back again, then yelled from the floor as he yanked at the bars. The kids' sessile determination moved me strongly.

Then I realized I was seeing everything wrong. Because on the tape I was walking toward the camera from the living room, which meant that Amanda had been filming. I was not the director but a subject. I bent at the barrier: "Hello, prisoners! Want a cake? A cake with a saw baked into it?" Addie had her hands atop the gate now, near the release, and we all gazed at one another.

Watching, I remembered that Amanda always let her shots run, alert to serendipities. Only well after the kids had stopped doing anything would she coax them to "Say goodbye! Say goodbye now, and wave!" Farewells to their future selves, intercepted by me.

Me with Addie and Walker, 2007.

Except for the unread set of James Fenimore Cooper, the Friend antiquities we possess—Grandpa Ted's ratty Persian rug and his mahogany dining table, which the kids loved hiding under when they were small—were picked out for me by Mom from Eugenia's estate. Mom didn't want any Friend bric-a-brac cluttering her house, but at Day's insistence the grandfather clocks slipped in. They remind him of his great-grandfather's compound and the tick-tock of the interminable velvet-draped Sunday afternoons. He intends that I get one and Pier the other, and that Timmie get the mantel clock.

It pains me that all that craftsmanship—the lunette, the moon dial, the winding hole and arbor—will get sold off. But my designated clock, which hasn't been wound for nearly a century, wouldn't fit in our apartment: there's no room for it in our mature design ethos. Amanda calls this aesthetic "cozy textured neutrals with a sense of heritage," and I call it "Amanda's aesthetic."

It was her idea to mix the Georgia mug shots in with photos of my ancestors, to graft some sass into my family tree. Her idea to replace the Knole knockoff with a low gray couch that blends better not only with the Buddhas, but with the Food52 merch that marbles the apartment, a trove of vases, candles, and cutting boards. And her idea to throw out the resin-handled flatware from our wedding registry. It was a little shiny, a little early aughts, and some of it was starting to rattle, but I loved it for its big, clunky practicality—those spoons held some motherfucking ice cream!—and as a talisman of the days when all we had going for us was big flatware. So when she came for the blue-and-white cow plates, I stood firm on principle. I just need to figure out what that principle is.

In the fall of 2019, a private equity firm bought a majority stake in Food52, allowing Amanda to cash out some of her equity. Suddenly, shockingly, we didn't have to check our bank balance every day. The knot of stress between Amanda's eyes slipped free; even her voice was lighter. We could travel more and work for our own satisfaction and repay ourselves for all the adventures we'd forgone! The only possession she craved was a car, her long-sought symbol of stability. So we got a Tesla and named it Bingo—a larky name we'd considered for Walker, years before. No more schlepping to Zipcar or Avis and then racing to get the car back on time! And setting Bingo's controls so it made farting sounds pleased us all beyond measure.

Once the financial pressure lifted, I realized that one reason I'd been aggrieved with Day was that I'd been counting on his money. My share of his estate would have doubled our retirement savings and banished the specter of the state nursing home, but in the last few years his savings had shrunk as they went toward his care. I felt hugely relieved not to have to think that way anymore, and ashamed that I ever had.

On the tapes, I watched Walker and Addie, at three, circle their room in their pull-ups screaming, "Squash ball, squash ball!" Addie brandished my squash racquet and Walker waved the case, bold as picaroons. Then she began yelling a fast, strangled "Twinkle, Twinkle"—"Sinker, sinker, little door!"—that sounded like Black Flag. I had forgotten how she attacked songs, even "Humpty Dumpty," as if she were about to plunge into the mosh pit. Walker was a performer, too, grabbing the mike at adult karaoke parties to croon "Baby Beluga." Where did all that go?

Immersed in these forgotten joys, I suddenly realized, with a drafty, door-ajar-somewhere sensation, that my ring finger was bare. I'd lost my wedding band. It wasn't on the ground, or nearby. I could barely tug it over my knuckle, so how could it have escaped me? But it wasn't in the bathroom, or the bedroom, or any room. In a full-body sweat, I retraced my movements for the past seventeen years, but it wasn't anywhere. It was just lost.

Amanda was playful and giddy, the old her, knocking loudly on my door, but I'd stopped answering. For years, I'd blamed my dissatisfactions on her and on the state of our bank account. Now the only person left to blame was me. But why do that when I could keep flailing about? Hurt people hurt people: the diagnosis that's also a handy excuse.

Not long after the investment, I began an affair with Martha. She was in her thirties and worked in publishing. We had similar backgrounds and she was smart and engaging and she hadn't quite figured out what she wanted to do with her life. Martha's youth made me imagine that she could see me fresh and that I might then somehow become fresh, become a new and better person. The Aslan fantasy.

We got together every few months in Philadelphia, when I went down to visit Day. Was it sordid to use visits to my dying father as cover for an affair? Yes. Was the affair also a way to deny that he was dying and that I was next in line? Yes, come to think of it. But I didn't require any fancy justifications; I had let my impulses take the wheel. When your car hits black ice and skids toward the guardrail, a floaty sensation exhilarates you for a moment, until you realize that you may crash or you may spin free but you can no longer steer.

Once the coronavirus pandemic hit and everyone locked down, our affair was conducted by text and phone for six months. Then we started meeting again, breaking Covid protocols, among other rules. We talked about Martha's job a lot, and I gave her advice, most of which she ignored because she wanted to make her own mistakes. We didn't talk about our future because I told her I intended to stay married. She wanted to know more about my marriage, to better understand where she stood, but I said that discussing Amanda and our life together felt like crossing a line. My boundary, as always, was not behavioral but informational.

Martha was going on dates, so I expected that sooner or later she'd find someone else. The dam would hold, and I could remain a cracked man who seemed, at first inspection, perfectly sound. If I framed the affair as *Trying to keep everyone somewhat happy*, it didn't sound so bad. I was doing mean things without meaning to, which is arguably worse than meaning to do them. At least villains have a plan.

When I arrived one evening, Day was in his leather lift chair. "Good morning," he muttered, as I settled beside him. His aides now used a Hoyer lift to transfer him between his bed and his chair; he dangled in the leather sling like a baby in a stork's beak. His chin was stubbly and he wore thick medical socks to prevent bedsores. He was watching highlights from Coco Gauff's run at Wimbledon a few months earlier on his bedroom TV; the channel looped them over and over. By the time the montage ended, he'd forget he'd just seen it.

After two more cycles of Coco, I turned the television off and began to fill him in on our doings. He didn't seem interested, so I remarked on the new lift chair and TV: "You finally got a man cave!" His surprised look made me realize I'd adopted the festive manner of a parent with a fractious child. I was Mom-ing him.

Hearing his aide in the kitchen, he asked, "Is that Baba?" Baba, who died in 2006, was Grandma Tim's cook: round and kind and flour-smelling. "Could you ask Baba for some ice cream?"

"I'll get you some in a sec," I said.

Day's pastor, Agnes Norfleet, had recently visited him and asked if he was ready to go. "No!" he'd cried. I wanted to understand his tenacity. Was it love for us? Love for the world? Or a lingering childhood fear born of Calvinism, which Muriel Spark defined as the "belief that God had planned for practically everybody before they were born a nasty surprise when they died"?

Out of habit, I began indirectly: "I was wondering what it means to you to be a Buddhistic Presbyterian." He looked blank. "That's what you told Timmie and me you were, last year."

"I don't know what I am," he said glumly.

"Nobody really does." I tried again: "Is there anything in the house you feel especially attached to—anything that carries particular meaning?"

"No." I suggested the clocks, the puppet, the frescoes, photos of him and Mom. "I don't remember much of anything." Day no longer knew what he didn't know—the very deficit he became a historian to combat.

"Can you recall any moments from your childhood? Or anything about your parents?"

He screwed up his face. "I remember a nurse discovering a gumdrop behind a thermometer."

"Why did that seem important to her? Or to you?"

"It's a very cloudy memory."

"Do you remember my story with the thermometer?" I

told him how I used to sick out in middle school by heating the thermometer under my reading light. "One morning, I heated the bulb too long. When you saw that my temperature was 108 degrees, you declared, 'Someone's been goosing this thermometer!'" He'd been so furious. Day's face was relaxing now, eager to get the point, so I explained, "Which was funny because your accusation was so indirect. Who else could that someone have been?"

He began to laugh, doubling over. Every few minutes, he'd think about it and start laughing again.

Amanda kept quiet when she filmed, more observer than choreographer, and she noticed details I missed. One morning she focused on Walker sleeping in his crib: "A close-up of his beautiful little feet. And his first bug bite." Her voice was full of wonder.

When I was away reporting, she narrated a tour of our apartment so the kids could see, when they were older, how we had lived. She lingered on the convict photos, explaining, "Most of them basically got brought in for drinking too much and then punching somebody." Panning to the Knole sofa, she said, "I have a strong love-hate relationship with it. Love the fabric, which you may hate. Hate the size! Which is too late to fix." Nostalgia; its binocular vision. "You guys are sweet little muffins, yes, you are," she told the kids. "You are making me very happy."

"Happy!" Walker repeated.

A few months later, I filmed her on that couch reading to the kids. They sat on her lap in their pj's. "'They left the house at half past nine in two straight lines'—one, two," Amanda said.

"Two," Addie agreed, pointing to herself and Walker.

" 'In rain or shine.' Where's the rain, guys?"

They cried "Rain!," pointing to Bemelmans's soft gray slants.

" 'The smallest one was Madeline.' "

"Mum!" Walker said, pointing.

"Yes, that's a tailor measuring her," Amanda explained. " 'She loved winter, snow, and ice. To the tiger at the zoo Madeline just said . . . ' "

"What'd she say?" I prompted.

"Poo-pooh!" Walker said. They all smiled at the danger so casually dismissed. The panache of it.

The second-to-last sequence was them, at five, dancing to "Don't Look Back," flailing around like protozoa. Walker, in a tank top, was going full Joe Cocker. The finale, a few weeks later, was their absorption in *March of the Penguins* on TV. Our penguins watching penguins. They turned as one to stare at me, aware of the oversight and not having it anymore, so I clicked the camera off for good.

That was, I think, the precise moment when the footage would have begun to really interest them later. When you become self-conscious, you become both much less happy— because you're no longer totally immersed in your waking life—and much more the person you'll be from then on. I wanted to keep drinking their life in, preserving it for them in some medium more capacious than memory.

After I watched Amanda read *Madeline* I woke at 2:18 A.M. with the realization—icy and terrible as middle-of-the-night clarities are—of my part in forming her carapace. Some of it, surely, derives from her hard-won CEO's resolve, and some is a reaction to the scuffs and scars of middle age. But I had repeatedly checked out, deserting her. And even when I was present, did I celebrate the haven she'd built for us? Did I encourage her tenderness at the sight of a baby or a small dog? When she tried on a new shirt and showed it off, twirling, did I try to see it through her eyes—*Who is this person she hopes to become?*—or did I just shake my head? Did I ever put her needs first, which she longed for and deserved above all things?

I married someone who would not leave me alone, which I wanted even more than I wanted to be left alone. Yet I'd meted out my generosity as if I had a limited supply, as if the glittering necklace of our days together were not collateral enough. This connubial strand.

After telling the thermometer story, I brought Day a bowl of ice cream, and he cheered up entirely. I told him I might play in the Canadian Nationals squash tournament.

"You should," he said. "You're probably at your peak."

"Well, I don't know. When was your squash peak?"

"My peak was at thirty-five."

"What about when you almost won the Nationals?"

"I should have won that. That was a second peak." He maneuvered a spoonful to his lips and began to chew. "I wonder if some people have a third peak."

"Are you planning one?"

"Oh, I'm thinking about it." The pauses were extending. "But some of the speed has come off my serve."

I told him that in Canada I'd be just over the border from Buffalo, so I could visit our house on Highland Avenue. "I wonder how small it will seem."

"Picayune," he said. He glared at the bowl. "Strawberry! I never liked strawberry." After another tortoise-like bite, he added, "Timmie got lost in Swarthmore."

"One day, or metaphorically?"

". . . Lost in that big house," he replied, several minutes later. It felt as if we were the twins in Einstein's relativity paradox: Day rocketed off at light speed and returned a moment later, from his perspective, to find me inexplicably much older.

"It seems like we found her, though," I said. He waggled his hand, the Italianate gesture he'd adopted as words began to fail him. I asked what was on his mind these days.

"Only that Trump is a chump. I'm not reading much." He gave a rattling sigh. "I am an ill-informed man."

"What would you like to be better informed about?"

"Sexual matters." He pursued the melting cream.

"Anyone's in particular?"

"Well, for instance, your life with Amanda."

"Uh-huh. Do you think about your life with Mom?"

"Oh, sure. We were together for a long time. If all my life's wisdom would come down to one axiom, it would be 'Choose carefully who you marry.' And that's not original." Worry creased his face. "She's been gone for a while, though."

"How long has it been?"

"A couple of weeks."

"That is a while," I said. "Where'd she go?"

His expression cleared. "She's traveling out west, visiting friends whose names I decline to pronounce."

"That sounds lovely. When will she be back?"

"This weekend." The thought comforted him. "Soon."

Planks

WHEN WALKER told me that he'd aced his history exam,
I encouraged him to pursue the subject, "like Grand-Day
did!"

"Not interested," he said.

"It can be pretty useful to understand what happened
before you came along. 'Those who forget the past are
doomed to repeat it,' you know."

"Yeah, I know," he said. Duh.

When Covid hit, and Day's caregivers wouldn't let us visit,
I often had the strange feeling that he and I were doing the
same thing at the same time: reading the paper, or writing a note, or lying awake in bed. In one of my favorite
novels, Thomas Harris's *Red Dragon*, the empathetic FBI
agent Will Graham feels a similar kinship with the serial
killer he's pursuing: the "sense that he and the Dragon
were doing the same things at various times of the day, that

there were parallels in the quotidian details of their lives."
Graham "viewed his own mentality as grotesque but useful,
like a chair made of antlers." I found my association of my
connection with Day to Graham's similarly grotesque, but
it also felt like a natural form of recognition. Growing up to
discover that you can't escape your parents is like walking
through a haunted house: you recoil, laugh uneasily—*Oh,
it's just me, in a mirror!*—and gingerly proceed.

The previous Christmas, Amanda had given me a set
of sessions at a meditation center called MNDFL, which was
casual about vowels and contemplative rigor. In a basement
in the East Village, surrounded by annoyingly flexible mil-
lennials, I was told, "Slouch on your cushion any old way
and entertain whatever thoughts come into your head,
venerable dude." To my surprise, I enjoyed the sitting and
the breathing and the noticing. During one soundbath, my
thoughts swirled in the gongwash until a chime reminded
me of the wind-chime sculpture at Maplewood that a
friend of Grandma Tim's had built from rusty flywheels,
levers, and hoes. When I was twenty, we took a family
photo posed around the sculpture. Everyone looked young
and glad, Mom and Day in the pink, all of us laughing
as Baba clicked the shutter. She was the one who shot
home movies of us: me in my flying saucer, spinning down
the hill.

I wished that I had home movies of Day, but I had his
letters. When I pulled them out, I was instantly reminded
that, contra the watchword of his youth, he had *everything*
to report. Yet I could see that he was troubled by his torren-
tial fluency. In an early note, he said he was pleased to have

been elected a "corresponding member" of the Geographic Society of Lima: "They have touched what may be my only talent, which is to correspond. Recognizing that gives me tremors of apprehension."

His letters often focused on squash battles won and lost, but I realized that this was at least in part owing to his awareness of my squid-like propensities. If he broached a delicate topic, he tried to leave me an escape route. After seeing the film *Sophie's Choice*, he wrote that "the young man who plays the narrator, 'Stingo' "—the circumspect Peter MacNicol—"reminds me somewhat of you in appearance, intellectual style, and faithfulness to his friends. I mean that as a compliment. (You can decide on your own time and in your own way if you care for the intended compliment or not.)"

The family in Woodstock, 1983, after Day left Swarthmore.

During the lockdown, Addison and Walker grew fearful about our health—particularly mine, as the family's silverback—and loath for any of us to leave the apartment. Terror management had shifted its focus from old people to other people. The days extended, interminable and interchangeable, until the applause for essential workers at 7:00 P.M. Addison and I would race to heave up the sash in the front window bay and clap and yell as windows and doors popped open up and down the street, a human Advent calendar.

I took up Pilates classes on Zoom, and came to appreciate a challenging pose called the ninety-degree bird dog plank. You do a kneeling plank and extend one arm sideways in the air and the opposite leg the other way, so you point in four directions, like a compass. *You can't take every path at once.*

One evening, as I prepared to work out, I saw in the mirror that my hair, uncut for months, curled over my headband like the fronds of a cycad palm. I looked weird yet naggingly familiar, like someone I saw every day. But who? Oh, yes: Psycho Dodo. He lay on Walker's bed alongside Bertrand and Bernard, beginning to be taken for granted.

We were all headed to Brooklyn Bridge Park, where I'd do my squash drills, ghosting on a patch of soccer field, Walker and Addison would kick a soccer ball, and Amanda would fast-walk circles around us. Then we'd return home to finish up: I was trying to knock out fifty straight push-ups and a four-minute plank on our bedroom rug. I'd crank Niall Horan's peppy "Nice to Meet Ya" on my iPhone, assume the position, and start sweating and swearing.

As we walked back, Addison pointed out a lilac band of sky over downtown Brooklyn. It was an eerie watercolor wash between the buildings and the black heavens, produced by humidity, or sodium arc lights, or aliens.

Two nights later, I noted that the lilac effect had returned. "No, Daddy!" Addison said. "That's just light pollution. Don't you know anything?"

"Clearly not. What else should I try to grasp before it's too late?"

She spread her arms and twirled: "Only everything."

In 1985, Day wrote me about visiting a close friend, the poet David Posner, who was dying of AIDS. Posner had been everywhere and known everyone; he declared that both Thomas Mann and Somerset Maugham had been in love with him in his youth. Now he could no longer speak. "So I reminisced about early days in Buffalo," Day wrote, "weekends in the country together with Cal Lowell; meals or drinks with Auden, Berryman, Stephen Spender." I'd have loved to hear more about these encounters with the giants of modern poetry, but it was the only time he mentioned them. Maybe because I hadn't responded.

Day recalled the time when David met us at Disney World, in the late seventies, and volunteered to take Pier and me on Space Mountain because neither Mom nor Day liked roller coasters (me either, since that day). "It was not the Magic Mountain, but some other kind of Mountain where you take god-awful plunges in a rail car. With Timmie too? I don't recall. But it was fun to be with him, wasn't it? Didn't we have fun?"

Three years later, he sent me a fan letter after I wrote a

piece for *Spy* under the name Celeste de Brunhoff; his note, mailed to the magazine, was signed "Sue D'Eaux-Nimbe." I remembered my astonishment at the pun: such a Mom move.

At the same time, he was reporting the breadth of his hotel rooms in paces—4, 2, even 1.5—the way a prisoner might. In 1991, he wrote from Brno, in what was then Czechoslovakia: "This is my tenth day of travel. I am a bit weary, a bit lonely. I feel more companionable with myself by writing you, and trying to imagine your reactions to some of the things I've seen and done." He craved more letters: "It is as much fun for me to receive as to send." Home alone, he wrote, "Sam"—Mom's Tibetan spaniel—"and I are holding things steady here. But it feels awfully empty." Mom, in a similar circumstance, had written: "Sam sends love. I've spent the entire weekend blissfully solitary, just with him."

Amanda heard a scratching sound in the kitchen wall and called me in. "It sounded like a squirrel," she said, pawing at the air. "Not quite as"—she gnashed her teeth—"as a rat." We listened tensely, but all was quiet. A few nights later, though, we both heard gnawing in the roof beams. The clothing moths were back again, too, fluttering everywhere as we angrily clapped and missed. During Covid our infrastructure grew oppressively needy: drawers squeaked, floors cracked, and cupboard doors sprang off their hinges. Everything seemed to require constant attention.

Amanda brought up the dog question one more time. We rehashed the cons: even as the house was falling apart, the kids kept forgetting to empty the dishwasher, do their laundry, and make their beds. So how much responsibility would they take for a dog? "On the pro side," she said, tentatively, "there's joy."

My letters from the last twelve years, after email swept the field, fit in one Amberg box. So I reread Day's dwindling correspondence out of order. In 2017, he wrote that a piece I'd done about the scientific quest for immortality was "the best article of yours that I've ever read." His handwriting was trembly, the lines not quite plumb. "But I know I may have missed the point. If you feel I have gone askew, just tell me so."

In 2016, he sent a postcard of a polar bear crouched over its paws in a sort of child's pose: "Thinking of you." I remembered wondering whether he was making reference to the polar bear card Mom had sent me years earlier, as a way of obliquely acknowledging the power of such consolations. I wish I'd asked.

The last letter I read was from 2014. Day had written me in mauve ink, noting that it was "not the ideal tint for male correspondence," but that his other pens had run dry. While conducting his periodic search for his letters to Mom, he'd turned up a wounding letter she sent him in 1985, "five pages detailing my shortcomings, that had struck me as coherent, yes, but incongruous and non-harmonious." He added that Mary had told him, " 'Remember what you loved about Elizabeth; and remember that she loved you.' *Good advice.* Trying to remember E. more fully, and not through the limited lens of that one letter, I turned to

your book, which I found wholly absorbing." He went on
to praise *Cheerful Money* handsomely, his past criticisms
forgotten or laid aside. This letter had startled me at the
time. Now I could see that his appreciation, and his implicit
apology, shouldn't have been so surprising. Like a detective
returning to a cold case, I was amazed by how much I'd
missed.

After five months of ghosting in Brooklyn Bridge Park, I
got much faster—or at least much more efficient at ghosting. I did some back-of-the-envelope math and decided I
was twenty-five percent fitter. The courts were still closed,
though. So what was it all for? There was a meditative, geo-
metric pleasure to the patterns: up, back, down, back, over,
back. But I was also spending time now to buy more time
later. Building a sort of wall, a defense not just against the
coronavirus, but against all diminishment. The sensible part
of me knew that I couldn't outrun decline, but I hoped to
make of myself a rear guard so mighty that death would be
hard put to overtake me.

When the world shifted to virtual engagement, the end
of every online meeting felt like a connection lost, a little
death. MNDFL went digital and then shut down, and my
poker group migrated onto PokerStars.net, with a Zoom
on the side for trash talk. This combination confused us
enough that Gil Schwartz, who almost always lost big, won
eighteen dollars. Gil, a recently retired writer and CBS
exec I'd known since my *Esquire* days, was in top form all
night, humming along to the Edith Piaf album playing
at his house in Santa Monica, zinging me for my under-

lit backdrop, a dark corner of my study—"How's it going, Nosferatu?"—and capping exchanges with a "That's what she said!" whenever it would seem especially dopey. His favorite form of humor was pretended stupidity. He kept going all in and for once he had the cards to back his bets.

Thirty-six hours later, he died of a heart attack.

I was on the couch in my study writing this book, when Amanda came in to discuss shopping for groceries. She broke off and peered into the corner behind me: "Oh my God!"

Certain it was a squirrel or a rat, I ducked away. "No, no!" she cried, and reached over me, blocking my view as I tried to turn back—marital Twister—then sprang out in triumph. Between her thumb and forefinger was my wedding ring.

Before we left town to spend a week at a hotel in rural Tennessee, I took out a few days' worth of garbage. Hoisting the heavy black bag over my shoulder, I trudged to the door, thinking, *Why doesn't anyone else ever take out the trash?* Amanda gave me a big wave: "Hello, Trash Santa!" I felt seen.

As we pulled away from the curb, Niall Horan's "Nice to Meet Ya" came on and Walker cried, "Oh my God!" and hit skip. I looked over in dismay, and he explained, "It's the new Sheryl Crow! Ten years from now, we'll hear it and it will seem so insignificant that you'll be ashamed you played it over and over and over."

"Maybe," I said, doubtfully. "We'll see."

We visited Day on the way down. Because of the virus, we sat masked on his bedroom steps, ten feet from where he bulked in his chair. He was amazed by how Walker and Addison had grown. "I wish I'd had more grandchildren," he said. "But I have no direct effect on that."

"You seem to have done pretty well working indirectly," I said.

"Grandchildren," he repeated, smiling at them. "Grand . . . children."

After the kids and Amanda went up to get ready for bed, Day and I talked a little about the Black Lives Matter protests. He thought they were a great thing. " 'Faith of our fathers, living still,' " he murmured, after a moment. " 'In spite of dungeon, fire and sword.' And Trump."

"What's that from?"

"A hymn I heard monthly—more than monthly—in prep school." He quavered: " 'O how our hearts beat high with joy/ Whene'er we hear that glorious word!' But they never say what that word is." He looked over anxiously. "What is the word?"

I scrolled on my phone. "It seems the word is 'faith.' 'Faith of our fathers! holy faith! / We will be true to thee till death!' "

He frowned, having forgotten about God. I hoped that God hadn't forgotten about him.

Every morning at breakfast at the hotel, a male cardinal, redder than the brightest poppy, rammed the restaurant's glass windows. He'd fall into the boxwood below, flutter back up, and repeat, over and over. *Bonk. Bonk. Bonk.* Then he'd fly to the glass door and try there. *Bonk.* I felt concerned, annoyed, and bewildered. Just around the corner from him, ten yards away, the restaurant's windows were wide open. The bird's behavior bothered me more than it should have—it seemed so pointless and self-defeating.

I decided, after no more than fifty or sixty bonks, that the cardinal was enacting my own project. But was that project my search for my father, or something else—something I hadn't quite figured out yet? *Bonk. Bonk. Bonk.* Dammit, the open window is *right over there.*

On Halloween, I got a text from Day's hospice social worker, Bonnie. She said that his speech was garbled, his skin was clammy, and his appetite was gone. "He didn't want me to read to him, just to sit with him quietly and hold his hand."

We drove down. As I entered his bedroom, he turned his head, found my face with his right eye, and said, "T . . . Ta . . . Taddio." His left eye was closed, the left side of his mouth drooped, and his left hand could barely squeeze mine. It seemed likely that he'd had a stroke. When Amanda came and sat beside me, he smiled: "Amanda." He turned back to me and his mouth worked, reconfirming: "Dad."

"Tad," I said.

"Yes."

I talked for a while about nothing important and he studied my face. Out on the lawn, we could see that his lofty Norway spruce, listing for years, had finally been cut down. Amanda said that the stump would make a handsome table.

Day's lips moved soundlessly. "Good idea?" I said. He nodded.

Amanda said she was going to the store: "What kind
of ice cream would you like?" Day whispered something.
"Black cherry?" she guessed. His good eye held her gaze,
then swiveled to my face, seeming to want to convey something less guessable.

Addison and Walker came in to sit with him, and Addison sang him the opening verse of the BTS song "Dyna-
mite." Then she read him a poem she'd just published in
her school newspaper:

Rapid
fading

Ragged petals
pristine thorns

Bloody breaths
peaceful deaths

A few minutes later, Day said, "I'm remembering your
poem." A whole clear sentence. I was burstingly proud of
both of them.

With the time line uncertain, we decided that Amanda
would go back to Brooklyn with the kids, and I'd stay.
Walker and Addison took turns holding Day's right hand
under the sheet and telling him that they loved him and
that he was the best grandfather. When they each lowered
his hand to say goodbye, he held tight and raised their clasp
up. I felt like I'd sprung a permanent leak.

The next morning Day could open his mouth to take morphine, but by the afternoon he couldn't swallow, and he was no longer responding to us. His right eye was fixed unblinkingly on the far window. Megan, his hospice nurse, said he'd probably had another stroke.

I called Timmie, who was planning to fly in from San Francisco with Scott and Lucia, and told her they should come ASAP. Pier and Sara were already on their way. I knew that once you stop taking liquids, you're near the end. Day's accessory-muscle breaths, those chesty gasps, were another sign. It helped to know these facts. And it didn't help at all.

Agnes Norfleet came to pray over him, brisk rites of commendation. Afterward, she found me sitting at his desk. Everyone was reporting to me, suddenly, as if my dispositions would make any difference. She said, "On my last visit, I had one of the most amazing conversations with your father that I've ever had with any human being. I asked him if he had any unfinished business, and he said, 'Yes.' I said, 'What?' And he said, 'I would like to write a Fifth Gospel.'" We both laughed. I could hear him saying that, delighted by his audacity. "I said, 'Well, what would that be about?' and he said, 'Jesus's sex life.'" She smiled. "And aren't we glad he didn't get the chance to write it?"

I had bugged Janice Duffin to make sure Day voted by mail, as the presidential contest in Pennsylvania was so close, and as I knew he'd take pleasure in helping to turf Trump out. The morning after Election Day the outcome was still uncertain, but Day was past all that. He was taking thirty breaths a minute, rapid, straining, whole-body breaths, and his hands and feet were icy. Mary shuttled in and out of his bedroom in an N95 mask, unable to settle.

Timmie unfolded the shutters by his bed to let in the sun. Pier picked *Family Laundry* from the bedroom bookshelf, opened it midway, and began reading. We all perched around the room, bearing witness. Pier's steady voice calmed Day and slowed his breathing, even during the self-accusing passage about Grandpa Ted: "I admit that I did not love my father as much as I should have. How much was that? More than I did anyway. How much could I have loved him? Infinitely more."

Megan checked Day's vital signs and said it could be anytime now. After she left, we took turns standing vigil. When I was alone with him, I wanted to say something, to utter some sweeping, healing remark, but I was at a loss for words. "I love you, Day," I finally said. He kept breathing. Then he stopped, and I thought he was gone. A mighty gasp, and he was back, fluttering against the window. I went to get my phone to text Amanda that she and the kids should come down again, and that was when he left us.

Two days later, we interred Day's urn just above Mom's, in the courtyard at Bryn Mawr Presbyterian Church. A thin panel keeps them apart together; two jars of olive oil. We retained half of his ashes to bury under the hydrangea in Wainscott, beneath Amanda's clay urn—the bush where Mom's ashes are part of the soil.

The grass was wet and the sky was gray. The work crew across the street turned off their leaf blowers so a minister we'd never met could say a few emollient words to the eleven of us and Mary. We played Alicia Keys's version of "Lift Every Voice and Sing" because Mary had said that Day liked that hymn, and because I hadn't yet found his funeral file. Then we got in our cars and drove back to his house, a ragged cortege.

We began to clean and sort and dismantle. We hired a realtor, turned off the phone and cable, forwarded mail, canceled subscriptions, alerted friends. There should be an app that alerts everyone when you're gone, one with a simple toggle: alive/dead. We were a chain of rheostats: when Day toggled off, we dimmed, too.

I kept thinking about the last time we'd been together with him, the previous December. On Christmas Eve, we'd trooped into his bedroom to read *The Tailor of Gloucester*, settling on the stairs and the chairs and the four-poster. Day sat up in his hospital bed, his hair freshly trimmed, wearing a blue velour sweatshirt that matched Mom's blue-and-white Ralph Lauren bedding. She bought the posy-patterned sheets and pillowcases—"hideously expensive but gorgeous!"—one at a time until she had the set, ignoring his complaints that she was turning their bedroom into a boudoir.

Scott passed Day the book for his turn and helped him put on his glasses. After dollying his arms to find the best focal length, Day began hesitantly: "The . . . father . . ."— the tailor, actually—"crossed the kitchen and stood quite still beside the dresser, listening, and peering through his spectacles." He was gaining strength, summoning it. "Again from under a teacup came those funny little noises—"

"*Tip tap, tip tap, tip tap tip!*" we cried.

After finishing on the tailor's lament—"Alack, I am undone, for I have no more twist!"—he nodded proudly and handed the story on.

Rising

TOO SOON, everyone had to get on with their lives. Pier would handle the estate's paperwork, Timmie would oversee selling the property, and I would return to Villanova every few weeks for two months to empty the house, to extract all the meaning we could before a cleaning service broomed out the last Christmas ornaments.

I hired Elizabeth Stahl to dispose of the books and to box and ship the items that each of us wanted—not so many, really. We sent a small truck to Long Island with Mom's bowfront dresser, love seats, and nested side tables, as well as twelve of her paintings and twenty-one boxes of family photos to sort through later. We were decanting her spirit to Wainscott, along with the maroon canister that held Day's ashes.

As Day had made me his literary executor, I set up camp in his study to go through his files. Starting with the bottomless cabinet on the north wall, I worked clockwise around the room. I found the family journal from our 1979 trip to Europe, in which I moaned about all the museum visits, sounding just like Walker. Then Day's letter to Mom from Dubrovnik: "You are my old city, my plum in flower, my moon, and my seven torches. You are the one I talk to when I talk to myself; and the one I long to hear talking." Then many more letters to her, as well as a few from her to him circa 1970 that were filled with endearments such as "I'm finding it difficult to sleep without you curled beside me." It was almost like they were still chatting in the next room.

The files revealed Day at every stage, from boy to old man, but there was a through line of irrepressibility. After eight ten-hour days, I was only halfway through, and being inside his head all day, inside the humming collider, was exhausting. But Day was inside my head, too. I kept being inhabited by memories of him inhaling through his nostrils and smiling determinedly, or trying to stifle a toothy grin— visitations in which he was my age. When I found the first file about his adulteries, on a day when I was going to see Martha, I felt sock-puppeted by an unwelcome hand.

We vexed an auctioneer by selling Day's coins and silver and clocks, his most valuable heirlooms, to a coin dealer, who outbid her. She grudgingly said she was still willing to sell a few of his remaining antiques. Then she arrived with two large moving trucks, and she and her crew tore through the house scooping up tables and paintings and dishware and stray shiny objects, including Amanda's coffeepot, and took off without leaving an itemized receipt. The ransacked house echoed coolly, accusingly.

Disorder encroached. As a historian, Day kept everything, but his zeal for a Dewey-decimalized order had given way, later in life, to an everything-pizza surrender: books and coins and ancestral cigarette cases were wedged into "Notes and Verses and Memorabilia, 1982–1985." I sensed his belief that the cabinets themselves would somehow sift and curate his work, causing the best to rise like cream, or like Christ. As if the cabinets—a fortress of steel against fire, theft, and premature discovery—were the citadel of God.

But as I discarded his bank statements and his tax returns going back to 1956 and his painstakingly revised drafts of obscure papers, I felt I was dismantling his life. Not elevating but erasing. I reminded myself that I was taking notes, crisscrossing his tracks with my own, and that he'd reconciled himself to the truth that every life reduces to ashes. "I do not flatter myself that anyone much cares about Dorie Friend, who lived from birth in the Great Depression (1931) to over 87 years until today," he wrote, in 2019. "An earnest loving, hard thinking, but by no means world-shaking lifetime. His greatest asset maybe was his assiduity—his written attempt to convey to others than himself this self as being more than an ass."

The Day I found here was a more curious, generous, errant, sensitive, bighearted man than the one I knew. But why, oh why, did he never share that part of himself with us while he was alive? Why leave it for me to find? Did he think we'd have an opportunity to talk about it later, in the heaven that I didn't believe in? Or had he intended to open the labyrinth, starting with those poems he sent me, before he lost the thread?

I couldn't accept that this vivid place I'd so often visited or turned to in my thoughts, this force field of mental reservation against which I'd pitted myself for so long, would soon disappear. That now I'd never be able to change his mind. I was skidding and spinning, the guardrail slamming toward me. Addison and Walker were already depressed by months of distance learning, and Day's death deepened their rut. Addison began to skip classes and fall behind, and Walker astonished Amanda and me, one afternoon, by bursting into sobs and asking if he'd ever feel joy again.

Finally, in January, only one pile remained: Day's last notes and letters, which he'd stacked on his desk. But it was time for the estate sale; I swept the pile into a box to take with me and began cleaning out his desk so we could include it. I found the fake Rolex, a squall of staplers, and a thick file devoted to Publishers Clearing House. Like his mother, Day had been thrilled to have already won. He'd overnighted his coupons to headquarters, then written increasingly crabby letters demanding his winnings. Suffering range anxiety about life, he was convinced that the grand prize would rejuvenate him. So where was it?

The estate sale proved to have the work-to-reward ratio of a lemonade stand. Day's Danish modern desk, his command post for sixty-five years, went for a dollar. I mean, c'mon, people!

That month, we got a puppy, a rust-colored Cavapoo. She weighed just three and a half pounds and had no idea what to bite or when to bark or where to pee. Her favorite foods were earplugs and hairbands, and she loved bellying under the dining table, the way Walker and Addison used to, and

refusing to come out. But she was an indefatigable licker of
ears and jumper onto laps and collapser into comic heaps,
and her tail wagged furiously when she saw us. We named
her Fiver, after the rabbit in *Watership Down,* but Addison
called her "The Child," as if we'd all had a baby. A walnut
swaddled in cotton batting.

I turned this book in while Day was alive. After he died, I
knew I had to revise it, but I didn't feel like revising it—
I didn't feel like doing much of anything. In March, four
months after his death, I finally began writing about his
files and his infidelities. But the book's new layer of candor
felt dicey. It felt bogus, because I was pretending I was better than him.

In June, Amanda read my new draft and told me she
felt differently about Day now, because he'd treated Mom
so badly: "It shocked me. And I couldn't believe he tried to
defend himself by saying it was only three women in forty-
three years!"

"You're right that he treated her badly," I said. "But I
still think it was a pretty good marriage, all things considered." She stiffened. *Why are you sticking up for him?*
"My mom could be remote and cold," I explained. Some
qualm behind my eyes made her think, *He's talking about
us.* Every time I wrote a book my most acute reader saw it
as a hostage video. My unconscious was trying to send her
a message, through blinks and furtive semaphores, that my
captors wouldn't notice.

The next morning, when I went around the corner
to play squash, Amanda opened my latest journal. When
she found me on the courts and knocked on the glass, her

expression made me think that someone we loved had died. I stepped out and she backed away. "I read your journal and I know about Martha," she said. She looked so stricken that I opened my arms, but she flinched and put up her hand. *This is bad,* I thought. And *I can't believe this.* And *What did I write?* And *I feel so exposed.* "Let's go somewhere we can talk," I said, and we stumbled out to a bench on the Promenade.

Amanda reminded me that I'd written about kissing Martha the first night she and I hung out, and that I'd felt smitten. I claimed that that was it, a kiss, that I'd immediately come to my senses. I was already feeling overwhelming despair and regret: it was suddenly, piercingly clear that the whole time I'd been fooling around I'd just been fooling myself—that only Amanda mattered. "Was there anyone else?" she asked. Her face held so much pain that I panicked and mentioned the old friend I'd made out with a few times in New York a decade back. In my dread, as my secrets churned in my throat—as I grasped the undoable nature of everything I had done—it seemed like a tenable stopgap. When we got home, I began frantically deleting any remaining incriminating texts and emails.

But a few hours later, when I was holed up in our bedroom doing I have no idea what, Amanda read more of my journal and discovered that I'd met Martha again a few weeks after that first night. She came in and refuted my lie, and the world spun so hard I fell off.

"Okay, yes," I said, "we had an affair."

For a moment neither of us could make sense of anything. Then Amanda screamed and said, "I can't believe this is happening." Tears poured down her cheeks. "You always complained that I never cried. Well, now you know how to make me cry."

Within twenty-four hours we somehow found a couples' counselor who was tough-minded, insightful, and warm. In our first session she gently said, "Your marriage, as you knew it, is over." This hit each of us hard, but it felt realistic. A few days later we told Walker and Addison that we were working something out with a therapist, that it was normal and healthy, and that we'd get through it. They seemed relieved, readier to believe this press release than Amanda was, because she knew more of the truth, and readier still than I was, because I knew all of it.

I repeatedly assured her that she'd done nothing wrong, that it truly was my problem, one I'd had long before we met and one that only got worse the more loving she was. But why should she believe me, the proven liar? I had never reckoned with the effect of Amanda's father's adultery on her, but now it added layers of lead to my blanket of remorse. Everything she'd thought I was—sturdy, loyal, and staunch—I wasn't. Relying on anyone is a perilous act of faith. Still, I'd occasionally see her eyeing me with an expression that mirrored mine: terror leavened with pity and love.

Five days later, Amanda was going to take Fiver for a walk, and I offered to go along. "Okay," she said, evenly. Leaving the apartment—a sultry afternoon, sun spilling through the maple leaves—felt like a first date. I had no idea what might happen. We hadn't done anything together except lie side by side every night, turning on twin spits of misery until 5:00 A.M., when she'd ask me the questions that had been keeping her awake. As we were crossing the suspension bridge to Brooklyn Bridge Park, Amanda threw her arms around me and said, "I'm hugging you on a bridge, Tad, because we're crossing a bridge into our future together." We embraced for so long that Fiver wound her leash around our legs, trying to get in on it.

Our therapist suggested we write a mission statement for our new marriage. We each drafted some ideas—they were pleasingly, touchingly similar—and merged them into a declaration. The middle part said:

> Moments of vulnerability will be treasured and encouraged. We will set aside time each day (the working idea is to do this before dinner) to stop, breathe, and check in. Not just "How was your day?" but "What's going on with you? What are you feeling excited or upset about? How can I help?"
>
> When one of us is stressed, or feeling anxious and alone, that person will strive to remember that we each know each other deeply. Trying to hide an unruly feeling doesn't actually hide it; it just establishes space between us. We will move toward distress and uncertainty, not away from it.

I wanted to tell Amanda that I was hiding more bad news. I had a vague plan to confess in a week or two, but I'd had a vague plan to do any number of menschy things. I was so grateful to her that I couldn't bear to threaten our recovery just yet. I knew that that's precisely *how* I would threaten it, but I kept convulsing at the thought, *She'll leave me. It's too much.*

In our couples' session a week later, I volunteered that when I went to parties I'd sometimes set out to charm, lighting up my Vacancy sign. Amanda found this more troubling than reassuring. When I was out that afternoon, she read deeper into my journals until she found the "boozy reunion" passage. She texted to ask who Phyllis was. The sky went dark, vacuumed of light. I called Amanda, shaking, and confessed the searing litany of infidelities going back to 2008.

Driving home, I half-expected to crash and three-quarters welcomed the idea. I found her on the couch in my study, devastated, surrounded by my journals and boxes of Kleenex. I sat and answered her questions, a man on death row with nothing more to lose. It was like seeing video evidence of a crime spree I'd gone on while sleepwalking. Everything I'd done repulsed me, and it was even more apparent to me now—and it had been extremely clear that morning—that I wanted only to save our marriage. So I had no good response to *Why?* and *How could you?* A misstep, even an affair, was one thing, but this was a pattern of betrayal for most of our marriage. Every family photo, every email I'd sent her from the road, every kiss of farewell or return—every kiss at all, really—now seemed to her stained with treachery.

That was by far the worst night of my life, our life. Worse even than when Mom died, because then everyone had suffered together and the blow had brought us all closer. Now Amanda was in agony because of me, and I was in agony because of me, and a lot of other people, friends and family and most of all Addison and Walker—*oh God*—would be stunned when they found out. "I don't think we can make it," Amanda said, two hours later. "It's too far to go."

The next day wasn't much better. If my responses to Amanda's questions were terse, she feared I was harboring further terrors; if I haltingly began to elaborate, it only confirmed them. Disbelief and embarrassment ate at her; shame and remorse at me. The twin boxes I'd built had detonated, leaving only a jagged wall of misery between us. I kept wanting to comfort Amanda, but my hands were the knives that had cut her. I couldn't settle on a guiding metaphor—every sensation was caustic yet fleeting—but I could feel the dismal texture of my future: the rented 1BR, the sad toaster oven, the alternate weekends. The terrible game of Invisible.

I started reading in my journals to see myself through Amanda's eyes. In those pages, she'd told me, I was insecure, petulant, frightened of change, and desperate for financial security but too entitled to go after it. I'd told her that I only wrote in my journals when I was feeling upset, so they were a fever chart of passing maladies. That was true as far as it went—but so what, because the journals were awful. Endless whining that my editor hadn't instantly read my piece, that other editors hadn't appreciated my genius, that the larger world hadn't genuflected before my work. Endless complaining about feeling shut out by Amanda with no recognition that I'd shut her out. So little wondering about my own role in my life, and so little appreciation or empathy or even curiosity about anyone else. My hallowed repository of rumination amounted to little more than an endless tantrum. I wanted to hurl the whole mewling sack of grievance into the trash, and myself after it.

The only thing that kept me going was that I felt so clear about my love for Amanda, and so scalded by the enormity of my behavior, that I knew I'd never cheat again. The idea of it made me feel ill. I told her that I wished she could inhabit my body to feel how I felt in every corpuscle, and to understand that the cozening voice in my head was silenced and that I could finally hear myself think and feel myself feel and know my own heart. She gazed at me for a long time, and for once it was hard to read her face.

Miraculously, Amanda didn't give up on me. Two nights after the bomb went off, she rolled toward me in bed and kissed me. Hating to see the misery in my eyes, she wanted to make me feel better. I know. I know. Whenever I think about it, I'm overcome. And I think about it a lot.

Miles of hard road lay before us, and it sometimes felt like we were crawling to it on our elbows. Amanda was not going to tolerate any more infidelities or live with the same man who'd committed them; I had to change. We had to recast our marriage, too, and make it new in more than name. We plunged into conversations and check-ins and three therapy sessions a week—Tuesdays at 9:00 for me, Wednesdays at 10:00 for Amanda, Fridays at 9:00 together—even as daily life amped up, too. There were crises with work, with our kids, and with Fiver, who began vomiting blood early one morning when we were fifty miles north of the city on our way to pick Addison up from camp. At times the cumulative pressure of being alive was almost too much.

To relax, we started watching TV together, a beloved habit we'd fallen out of. The night before Amanda gave birth, we'd stayed up till 3:00 A.M. watching *Pride and Prejudice*. But every series we chose, from *The White Lotus* to *The Morning Show* to *Ted Lasso*, had an affair plot. We'd both tense at the first hint of betrayal: *Really? Another one?* Yet these jarring reminders were also useful, in their way, because they made clear that my secret was just a predictable plot point on the whiteboard of every show in production: the C-story husband who precipitates a crisis. I was not even an original asshole, an outlier asshole. I was just another schmuck.

Because I'd driven Martha in Bingo, Amanda refused to get in the car again—it symbolized everything I'd spoiled. Trading it in for another model helped a little. And making love helped a lot. It was like suddenly getting cable and discovering that there are a thousand channels out there. We began locking the door to our bedroom, and Addison said, knowingly, "I heard you giggling in the bathroom!" Our newfound ardor—the best and most passionate sex I'd ever experienced—made it clear what our marriage could be. There were mornings now when Amanda would sip her coffee and turn to me with a smile, and I'd feel a blood surge of gratitude. How had I never appreciated the full radiance of her beauty and courage and humor and sensitivity and integrity?

Still, neither of us could sleep for more than a couple of hours. And PTSD kept hitting us, day after day, knocking us back into fight-or-flight mode. I grew to dread the clammy palms, the racing pulse, the sensation of inexorable doom. In one couples' session I felt so overwhelmed by all that I'd done that for a full minute I could mutter only a strangled "Sorry . . ." I was in the dark, in the hole, manacled to a wall in a prison colony where even the possession of words was forbidden. *I don't want to use words the same way anymore anyway.*

*   *   *

In the mid-nineties, traveling in Cambodia, I picked up a tapeworm. By the time the problem got diagnosed two months later, when I was gagging from acid reflux and had lost twelve pounds, it was dozens of tapeworms. "You have a very large worm load," the doctor said, which is not the sort of compliment you want to hear. A pill the size of a bullet killed them all. They tumbled out my anus and I stared at them for a while before flushing the toilet. How had that writhing boil of parasites been festering inside me?

As I write this, I keep wanting to expel the shame load in my belly. If only there were a pill for it.

Could this be the pill?

As we'd be spending August in Wainscott, we set Zoom calls in early July with Timmie and Scott, and separately with Pier and Sara, to explain why we might seem off. I told them what I'd done and that I was entirely to blame, and Amanda added that all we needed from them was understanding. Everyone was very supportive, but we both felt low afterward. Timmie had seemed completely thrown, and Sara's mouth had dropped open and stayed open. We'd done a hard thing, but it had just upset everyone—and it hadn't fixed our marriage.

We took Addison and Walker to Southern California for two weeks, roaming from Santa Barbara to Laguna Beach. Getting out of our apartment, away from that muggy interior weather, opened us up. Jokes seemed funnier, suddenly, and even toast tasted better. We skeeved the kids out by kissing in the car, by the pool, on the exercise bike, and at the ostrich farm.

When Amanda's sister Rhonda, whom Amanda had confided in about my betrayals, joined us in Santa Monica, I
asked her to get a coffee with me. I apologized for hurting
her as well as for devastating Amanda. Rhonda accepted my
apology, thoughtfully, then fixed me with a man-up stare
and said, "Do better!" I was trying to. I'd always secretly
thought I was right about pretty much everything, and it
was humbling to discover that I'd been so comprehensively
wrong. Like a Jain, I didn't want to hurt anyone anymore,
not even an ant.

Some days this felt like a big ask. I was so accustomed to
being funny and writing sharply and keeping everyone at
a certain remove, so accustomed to filling up my tank with
high-octane self-pity and roaring off down the wrong road,
and then to complaining (but only to myself) that I had
gotten so lost because I'd been willfully misled. *Happy is
the man that has no autobiography.* But even when I felt so
rotten that I wished Amanda had never read my journals, I
was glad she had. Being exposed was a necessary precursor
to being seen. And now that I was visible to Amanda—and
myself—I had to grow up.

I did wonder what would be left once I threw off my
knobby shell. Like a hermit crab making the precarious
naked scuttle, I had no idea what my new home might look
like. One afternoon I asked Amanda what my strengths
were, and she wrote a list:

- Fierce competitiveness that inspires you to push
  yourself really hard with things that interest you like
  squash
- Underlying sweetness and vulnerability

- Superior listener
- Caring and loyal friend
- Forgiving of people's flaws
- Intelligence
- A-level hugger

There was an understandable hole where my qualities as a husband might have been celebrated, but it was a reassuring array.

What if, I wondered, my new home was my old home, only seen on a different wavelength? I decided to resolve every marital issue by asking, *What would make Amanda happy?* This shift in mindset—the goal of marriage, after all—began to make a real difference in our daily life. When she suggested changing our Christmas plans after we'd begun making them, and I rolled with it instead of roaring like a wounded grizzly, her eyes went wide. Maybe it wasn't too late for me to bloom.

During the last couples' session on our trip, over Zoom from our Santa Monica hotel, Amanda expressed her fury at all the things she'd never know that I'd said to and done with other women, at all the parts of me that she was being asked to trust, on thin evidence, would not destroy her again later. At all I'd kept hidden. Welling with remorse, I promised it would never happen again. After the session, we rocked together on the couch. Then she looked at me—that penetrating gaze—shivered as if she were boarding a plane, and said, "I'm all in."

"I'm all in, too!"

*   *   *

In Wainscott, I borrowed Amanda's wedding ring. Then I sent both our rings to a jeweler to have ALL IN and the date we'd declared it, 7/26/21, inscribed on their interior bands. Each of us took a separate walk with Timmie and caught her up, bringing her back to us. And then we began to relax. We spent hours negotiating a brutal croquet course that Pier had constructed among the trees, one snarled with roots and stumps and potholes. We played tennis and Taboo and bodysurfed and began to sort through the boxes of family photos and had long, discursive dinners around the big new table. Even the geese overhead seemed to be chorusing squawky approval. It was the best August in years.

A model for our new marriage was near at hand. ALS had stifled Sara—she used a wheelchair all the time now, and her speech was slow and effortful—and it was awful and arbitrary and unbearable. Yet she bore it. Amazingly, she laughed harder and more easily than ever, blazing with an unquenchable radiance. Pier drove her to New York for her drug infusions and fed her bites of cut-up food and massaged her cramping fingers, remarkably attentive and loving. His previous impatience with setbacks and illogic had been baked out. One morning, as we walked to the tennis court (we won the doubles again, unaccountably), I said how impressed I was by his and Sara's serenity. "Even more than a year ago, you both seem—"

"—like we were made for ALS?" He laughed, without bitterness. He was a different piece of the Day puzzle than I had believed him to be. The boyish, resolute part that naturally behaved well. Or maybe Pier was just my brother.

Maybe, now that we'd scattered the last of Day's ashes, we could finally remove him from our equation.

That ceremony, one gray afternoon, had been solemn and satisfying. Everyone took a handful of Day in turn and knelt beneath the hydrangea to pat him into the earth with Mom. The chalky white ash clung to my hands. Even after I washed up for several minutes, a full surgical scrubbing, I could still feel his tenacious residue.

Our emotional plunges continued. The unfairness of so many demands being made of Amanda after she'd been so wronged often made her sad or angry or even hopeless. But when we talked—hearts rabbiting, eyes wide—we could hear each other now. I still didn't always believe that I deserved her. But on the upswings, because my feelings were no longer just about me but about us, I felt so much better than I ever had. I was passable at intimacy! Maybe even promising!

At the end of the month, Amanda and I went for a walk on the beach before dinner, skirting the high-tide selvage of tiny crab shells. We were walking together nearly every day, tugged rapidly onward by Fiver. I'd told Amanda I'd even go for a fast walk, but she generously hadn't taken me up on it. Near the jetty, which was being pounded by the swell from a distant hurricane, I knelt in the sand and slipped her engraved ring onto her finger, enjoying her surprise. I promised I'd be loyal to and intimate with and worthy of her, for keeps.

Just before we returned to Brooklyn, Amanda came out of the shower pink and bright-eyed and whispered in my ear, "This is what I always hoped our marriage could be."

This unchanging place had helped us to change, to log a new set of pencil marks on the doorframe. Or maybe it had just helped us measure our changes, and being there felt so different, suddenly, because we sensed the sand running out of the hourglass. The late-afternoon light astonishes because it does not last. Twenty more summers to appreciate all that we have? Thirty, if we're lucky? Beneath the red cedar, duff and dirt have sifted over the REMEMBER stone, effacing it letter by letter, and soon MEMBER will become EMBER.

Me and Amanda, fall of 2021.

Fiver likes to sit in our front window bay, the same window Addison and Walker used to run to after a trip, and sniff the air as she watches the life below. Then she turns her head to peer at us, her expression so sagacious we half-expect her to start telling our fortunes. On my birthday this fall, we all ate generous slices of Amanda's Dump-It cake, and Fiver scampered among us giving licks of comfort as Addison played "Riptide" on her ukulele, her smoky voice purling low:

> *Lady, running down to the riptide*
> *Taken away to the dark side*
> *I wanna be your left-hand man*

I was swamped by an immersive sensation I thought I'd lost, a meniscus of feeling that shimmered and brimmed over. Amanda and I exchanged a lingering smile at the abundance.

Addison, who'd streaked her hair bright red as a kind of battle flag, told me, "I think I love Fiver *too* much."

"Loving anyone too much is not really a thing to worry about," I said.

"But I'm going to miss her a ton when I'm in college."

"Which will bring you home—our secret plan."

"Oh, I'd come home anyway. Probably." Her deadpan has improved considerably.

Walker met the rampant disorder with a furrowed brow. He wasn't sure he was ready for Fiver, even having yearned for her so. Was she too much? Absolutely! He began to accept pandemonium as his lot. One day, heating up ramen for lunch, he turned from the stove with his old smile and announced, "I am so ready for adult life!"

They seem strong enough to cope when we fill them in

on the whole story. I dearly, dearly hope they are. But it's too soon to tell.

When I looked through Day's papers from his desk, I found that he'd written me a final letter. He'd dated it, in small, shaky handwriting, "Sunday April?," then folded it into an envelope that he'd stamped and addressed, but forgotten to send.

For years, I'd thought of our relationship as a one-way dynamic: he hiding, and I seeking. Then it became bruisingly clear to me that I'd been hiding, too. Now, as I read his letter, I knew for sure that he had also been seeking.

Dear Tad,
Ever since you mentioned Ejaz Rahim the other day, I've been thinking about him. And you.

I've misplaced my glasses and I don't see too good. But I hope I can last until the letter is over.

In my mind, I play the jazz from "High Society" over and over.

I know this letter is higgledy-piggledy, but that's all I am capable of.

I love you. That's why I write.

All I remember about Ejaz Rahim is "under average American height," dark hair, and dark complected. I know he's much more complex than that, but I don't have words for it. Tell me about him!

It was lovely having you all here for a day. All of you. All the time.

I love you (repeat).

Day

The door had closed, but he'd kept the window open.

Acknowledgments

My agent, Binky Urban, has been my friend and advocate for three decades. Gillian Blake at Crown had a vision for what the book could be and was admirably patient as I tried to get it there. Thanks also to Amy Li, Matthew Martin, Michele Park, and Robert Siek at my publishers for their sharp-eyed assistance. David Remnick was a generous champion of this and numerous other projects. Sharon Berger provided lifesaving support in a time of great need. And I am indebted to Dan Algrant, Rich Appel, Deborah Copaken, Deborah Needleman, Kathryn Schulz, Franny Taliaferro, John Tayman, and Nick Trautwein for helping me to improve the manuscript.

Most of all, I am profoundly grateful to my wife, Amanda. But for her, this book would not have been possible.

About the Author

Tad Friend is a longtime staff writer for *The New Yorker* whose work has appeared in *The Best American Travel Writing*, *The Best American Sports Writing*, *The Best American Crime Reporting*, and *The Best Technology Writing*, among other collections. In 2020 he won the James Beard Award for Feature Reporting. His memoir, *Cheerful Money: Me, My Family, and the Last Days of Wasp Splendor*, was chosen as one of the year's best books by *The Washington Post*, *Chicago Tribune*, *San Francisco Chronicle*, and NPR. He lives in Brooklyn with his wife, Amanda Hesser, the founder of Food52, and their twins, Walker and Addison.

Twitter: @tadfriend